ADVANCE PRAISE FOR
Riding the Fifth Wave in Higher Education

"James Ottavio Castagnera has 40 years of legal practice and university administrative experience. He brings that knowledge and wisdom both to the classroom, at Drexel University's Kline School of Law, and to this thoughtful book. His lifetime of experience makes him exceptionally qualified to opine on the present state of American higher education."—DANIEL M. FILLER, Dean and Professor of Law, Drexel University, Thomas R. Kline School of Law

"As a counselor to colleges and universities on some of their most pressing legal issues for approximately 20 years, I have a dedicated place on my desk for *Riding the Fifth Wave in Higher Education*. An invaluable resource on higher education, James Ottavio Castagnera approaches each problem through a combination of legal training and more than 30 years of university administrator experience. The results are solutions that are fundamentally sound, easy to grasp, and highly practical. For an understanding of current issues from someone on the front lines, this is the book you should turn to first."—ANGELO A. STIO III, Partner at Pepper Hamilton

"In his important new book, James Ottavio Castagnera analyzes the current fierce wave of change in higher education driven by market economic forces, income inequality, technology, and the transformation of higher education from a social value into a commodity. The book should be read by everyone interested and concerned about the state of higher education."—WILLIAM A. HERBERT, Executive Director, National Center for the Study of Collective Bargaining in Higher Education and the Professions, Hunter College, City University of New York

"James Ottavio Castagnera traces four stages in the evolution of higher education in the United States and provides the rationale for a fifth stage (wave) fueled by technology and the Internet resulting in a long-anticipated and forecast consolidation of providers (to borrow a term from the health care industry) and ascendancy of career and professional curricula at the expense of those disciplines that instill critical thinking fundamentally important to a citizenry capable of fulfilling its role in a vibrant democracy. The author provides a summative business-model analysis and recommendations for surfing the Fifth Wave that will rankle some, and if pursued, would have profound collective bargaining implications on campuses, both private and public, with faculty bargaining units. *Riding the Fifth Wave in Higher Education* is illuminating and instructive reading for anyone with an interest in the forces that have shaped and continue to drive the evolution of American higher education in general and private-sector higher education in particular."—JEFFREY CROSS, Co-Editor-in-Chief, *Journal of Collective Bargaining in the Academy*

Riding the Fifth Wave
in Higher Education

This book is part of the Peter Lang Education list.
Every volume is peer reviewed and meets
the highest quality standards for content and production.

PETER LANG
New York • Bern • Frankfurt • Berlin
Brussels • Vienna • Oxford • Warsaw

James Ottavio Castagnera

Riding the Fifth Wave in Higher Education

A Survival Guide for the New Normal

PETER LANG
New York • Bern • Frankfurt • Berlin
Brussels • Vienna • Oxford • Warsaw

Library of Congress Cataloging-in-Publication Data

Names: Castagnera, James, author.
Title: Riding the fifth wave in higher education: a survival guide for the new normal /
James Ottavio Castagnera.
Description: New York: Peter Lang, 2018.
Includes bibliographical references.
Identifiers: LCCN 2017028852 | ISBN 978-1-4331-3372-5 (hardback: alk. paper)
ISBN 978-1-4331-3371-8 (pbk.: alk. paper) | ISBN 978-1-4331-4705-0 (ebook pdf)
ISBN 978-1-4331-4706-7 (epub) | ISBN 978-1-4331-4707-4 (mobi)
Subjects: LCSH: Education, Higher—Aims and objectives—United States.
Education, Higher—United States—Finance.
Universities and colleges—United States—Finance.
Universities and colleges—United States—Administration.
Education, Higher—Effect of technological innovations on—United States.
Classification: LCC LA227.4 .C38 | DDC 378/.01—dc23
LC record available at https://lccn.loc.gov/2017028852
DOI 10.3726/b11606

Bibliographic information published by **Die Deutsche Nationalbibliothek.**
Die Deutsche Nationalbibliothek lists this publication in the "Deutsche
Nationalbibliografie"; detailed bibliographic data are available
on the Internet at http://dnb.d-nb.de/.

© 2018 Peter Lang Publishing, Inc., New York
29 Broadway, 18th floor, New York, NY 10006
www.peterlang.com

All rights reserved.
Reprint or reproduction, even partially, in all forms such as microfilm,
xerography, microfiche, microcard, and offset strictly prohibited.

This book is dedicated to my son, Marc James Castagnera, a Hamburg investment banker, and my son-in-law, Corey Holland, a Hollywood videographer and actor…two young men who are making their own waves.

CONTENTS

Introduction   1

Part One: The Challenges

Chapter 1. The Five Great Waves: An Overview   5
Chapter 2. The Fifth Wave: A Deeper Dive   19
Chapter 3. The Decline and Partial Resurrection
of Public Higher Education   31
Chapter 4. The Decline and Crippling of For-Profit Higher Education   43
Chapter 5. The Decline of Not-for-Profit Higher Education   69

Part Two: Some Possible Solutions

Chapter 6. Addressing the Cost of Instruction   91
Chapter 7. Addressing the Facilities "Arms Race"   101
Chapter 8. Capitalizing on a Potential Window of Regulatory Relief   111
Chapter 9. Some Real-World Solutions   127

INTRODUCTION

At least for me, 2015 went down as the watershed year. The year began with Sweetbriar College, a tiny school for women in northern Virginia, announcing it intended to close its gates in June, only to be hauled into court and ordered to remain open. Next came the gutting of once mighty Corinthian Colleges by the U.S. Department of Education, leaving some 16,000 current enrollees wondering where that left them…other than saddled with student-loan debts and lacking diplomas. Next, the U.S. Department of Justice indicted the CEO and CFO of ITT, another major player in the for-profit sector of American higher education, for fraud.

The drumbeat of institutional destruction rattled into the ridiculous, when a for-profit business school in north Jersey—revealed as recruiting the homeless into its student body—threw in the towel.

Meanwhile, further south in the Garden State's mid-section, my own institution—a private, not-for-profit university of some 4,000 students and 600 employees—was just coming off its Sesquicentennial celebration and sustaining an operating deficit for FY 2015–2016. After announcing a third year of no raises for its staff, along with a cut in pension contributions, and negotiating a new contract with AFSCME containing similar flat wages for its clericals, the administration turned to the faculty for additional relief.

When the American Association of University Professors, which has represented the faculty, librarians, and coaches since 1974, declined to proffer any concessions in midcontract, the president and his cabinet pulled the trigger just days prior to the October 31st deadline for declaring a faculty layoff… the first in the 40-year collective bargaining relationship. The announcement at a "town meeting" attended by perhaps 80 percent of the workforce ignited a predictable firestorm of protest from faculty and students alike. Fourteen programs were targeted for closure with a concomitant release of a like number of full-time faculty, some tenured, and a somewhat larger number of adjunct teachers, some with seniority rights.

The president and trustees weren't bluffing. But they did welcome the union's capitulation. Significant wage concessions, combined with an excision from the collective bargaining agreement of several onerous articles that stifled innovation, resulted in a rescission of the furloughs and closings…at least for the time being.[1]

A dozen years earlier, I had published a journal article entitled "The Next Great Wave in American Higher Education." In it, I charted four earlier waves of innovation in our industry, beginning with the founding of liberal arts colleges as early as colonial days, progressing through the establishment of the great public land systems starting soon after the Civil War, followed by the creation of the equally distinguished and influential private research universities bearing telling names such as Carnegie-Mellon, and finally the megaversity movement of post-WWII.

My article postulated—not an original prognostication, I grant you—the fifth great wave, a wave generated by new technologies, most notably the computer and the Internet. Twelve years later, that wave has broken upon our shores and, like the tsunamis so powerfully presented in several recent feature films, this wave is threatening some edifices of higher ed once thought impervious to such changes in the environment of our enterprise.

This little book is aimed at assisting my colleagues, who must keep their heads above the maelstrom or drown, in understanding the onslaught they face and, I hope, in their coping successfully with it. Survival is the imperative, smooth sailing the ideal.

Note

1. These events and their sequel are recounted in greater detail in Chapter Nine.

Part One
The Challenges

· 1 ·

THE FIVE GREAT WAVES

An Overview

Four distinct epochs or waves can be discerned in the history of higher education. This chapter argues that a fifth wave, perhaps the most revolutionary of all, is currently cresting, posing a unique challenge to higher education administrators and faculty. The four previous waves can be summarized briefly as follows:

- In the 85 years between the Declaration of Independence and the Civil War, some 800 liberal arts colleges sprang up across the United States. My own alma maters are typical. Franklin & Marshall College owes half its name to a modest amount of seed money donated by the great Benjamin Franklin in 1787. Case Western Reserve University first saw the light of learning as Western Reserve Academy. "The undergraduate college took…the essential step necessary for a broad education for general citizenship.…These institutions were of a size and scale that could be created by a group of private individuals—not requiring great fortunes or state support" (Cox, p. 14).
- The end of the Civil War until the turn of the last century was the era of the great land-grant institutions. This expansion of higher education led to the first shakeout. "By 1900, only 180 of those first 800 small colleges remained active; larger, subsidized state universities consumed

market share by offering more educational services, subsidized prices, and often more pragmatic and career-oriented curricula" (Cox, p. 14).
- Around the turn of the last century, the third great wave broke upon the shores of higher learning. Wealthy industrialists such as John D. Rockefeller (The University of Chicago), Andrew Carnegie (Carnegie Mellon University), Cornelius Vanderbilt (Vanderbilt University), and Leland Stanford (Stanford University) founded high-quality, private universities. The institutions were often world class in their curricula, faculty, and architecture, importing many of these elements from their great European counterparts. Thus, with Chicago, "Cambridge inspired the architecture, while Berlin inspired the pedagogy and faculty structure" (Cox, p. 14).
- Fast forward yet another 50 years, and we see the GI Bill and the postwar technology boom, fueled in part by the Cold War, driving the creation of the "megaversity." This term is commonly used to describe a variety of large institutions, all of which share at least the following characteristics: faculty numbering in the thousands and student bodies numbering in the tens of thousands; sprawling and/or multiple campuses containing a large number of undergraduate, graduate, and professional schools and colleges; and a large and cumbersome administrative bureaucracy overseeing these complex operations. (We have also seen the proliferation and maturation of the community college. However, in this chapter, I will limit my focus principally to four-year institutions.)

In all, then, we can identify four distinct waves of institutional development in American higher education, each of which spanned about a half century of American history.

The fifth wave is breaking. "The age of the Internet and other new media forms is giving rise to a new wave of institution building, right before our eyes.... Ours is an extraordinary moment in history" (Cox, p. 17). What is it we may expect to observe and experience among the phenomena of this new era? Among the main indicia of this new wave are the following:

- There will be a shakeout of weaker institutions as the current disruption leads inevitably to a concomitant contraction.
- When the shakeout is complete, higher education will not be populated exclusively by e-educators. Nor will the landscape of higher education boast only the largest and wealthiest bricks-and-mortar institutions. Rather, as in the past, we should anticipate a mix of liberal arts colleges,

land-grant universities, and wealthy private universities, including megaversities, coexisting in rationalized competition with the e-educators and other for-profit entrants of this 21st-century wave.

What do these predictions portend?

- The wealthiest among us need not worry about this latest wave of change. For example, with something like $20 billion in endowment money and a reputation second to none, Harvard University has a secure position. An apt analogy might be to the oil industry. At the turn of the last century, Standard Oil was the most powerful corporation in the United States and Rockefeller was its wealthiest citizen. Despite the government's antitrust suit 100 years ago against Standard Oil, our love affair with automobiles ensured a powerful position in corporate America for the Seven Sisters, those seven corporations, including Mobil and Chevron that succeeded Standard Oil in settlement of the suit.
- At the opposite extreme are institutions that might be no more than one or two bad-freshman enrollments away from closing their doors. For these, daring solutions make sense. With little to lose, risk taking is their best bet.

For the rest of us—the overwhelming majority of traditional institutions of higher learning, which are neither assured of success nor in imminent danger of failing—the observations of Fernand Braudel may be worth noting. One of the world's leading economic historians, he stated the following concerning the waves of prosperity and poverty that have buoyed up and sunk nations: "The moral of the story is that a loss is never the result of a single throw—nor indeed is a triumph. Success depends on seizing the opportunities of a given period, on doing so time and time again, and piling advantage on advantage" (Braudel, p. 50).

Colleges and universities are often the targets of criticism, particularly from would-be or actual corporate partners, for the slowness of decision processes. But corporate America has come in for criticism from its counterparts in Japan and Germany for just the opposite trait—too much attention to a single quarter's profits as against long-range planning and performance.

We might very well reflect upon the possibility—dare I say, the probability—that we are only at the very start of this next wave of change, a wave that will wash over higher education and ebb around the middle of the new century. We also might consider that while the weakest members of the herd will fall and perish, representatives of every species—liberal arts college, land-grant institution, private university, megaversity—will survive as part of the new higher education landscape. And survival may depend upon adopting medium- to long-range strategies, rather than racing after quick fixes.

My belief is that the majority will survive. What leads me to this conclusion, rather than the conclusion that the decline of small liberal arts institutions in the second wave will be proportionately repeated? At present, only one percent of the world's population holds college degrees. In this Information Age, the world's uneducated masses will look to the United States to meet an enormous, pent-up demand. There will be plenty of "customers" for everyone. And while many millions will want the convenience of learning at a distance, millions more will continue to buy a traditional product or some combination of the two. Therefore, there is ample room for all of us to ride the new wave of change. With good medium- to long-range strategies, which match historical mission, current strengths, and particularized opportunities, we all have a chance to land safely on the beach by mid-century.

The Second Wave: 1865–1900

The period 1820–1896 has been termed "The Victorian Equilibrium":

The new change regime might be called the price equilibrium of the Victorian era. It coincided almost exactly with the life of Queen Victoria herself (1819–1901), and was closely linked to the cultural values that she represented. Its character was most clearly evident in Great Britain. Prices in that nation fell sharply from 1813 to the early 1820s, and then fluctuated within a fixed range for more than fifty years. They fell again during the depression of 1873, and stabilized once more until nearly the end of the 19th century. There was no sustained inflation in Britain from 1820 to 1896 (Fischer, p. 156).

In the United States, the Civil War stimulated an inflationary spike that disrupted this equilibrium. For the failed Confederacy, the spike was one of hyperinflation. But the war's aftermath was characterized by deflation; by 1880, the 1861–1865 inflation had been wrung right out of the U.S. economy (Fischer, p. 157). During the latter half of the 19th century, "[l]ong-term improvement was the rule for both highly skilled artisans and farm laborers" (Fischer, p. 160).

Although depression engulfed the Western world in 1873, from about 1876 onward, a "public health revolution" caused death rates to decline dramatically (Fischer, p. 186). The effect was a general rise in world populations, with the United States getting much more than its share due to immigration. While Rockefeller was building Standard Oil and revolutionizing the way American business operated in the eastern part of the country (see Yergin, chapter 2), East Coast cities, notably New York, were bulging and bustling (Kazin, p. 257).

Among the notable developments of this era were the great land-grant institutions, the genesis of which may be seen from an examination of the career of John Wesley Powell, best remembered as the explorer of the Colorado River (see Worster). Powell's achievements were supported mostly by government largess, as were the land-grant institutions, including the future University of Illinois, with which he enjoyed an early affiliation. Powell was the son of immigrants whose story typifies that of millions who came to America during the 19th century. Combining an old-world trade (tailoring) with attempts at farming, the family moved from upstate New York to the Midwest. There they bought, developed, and sold a succession of ever-larger tracts of rural land, building their nest egg, until they finally retired in modest affluence to Wheaton, Illinois, by about the time of the Civil War.

The founding of the town, a bit northwest of Chicago, is a typical tale not only of American frontier society but also of American higher education in that early era.

A conference of Wesleyan Methodists meeting in Batavia, Illinois, in 1851 resolved to create a new comprehensive school and college under church auspices—an Oberlin for the prairie. Two brothers named Wheaton stepped forth to offer forty acres of land for a campus in the new town they were platting, a town bearing their name. They conceived of a Christian community free of alcohol, with a Christian school at its core. The conferees readily accepted their offer, for the location was ideal. The new town of Wheaton lay on the outskirts of Chicago in DuPage County, 25 miles west of the city's Michigan Avenue, and the Galena and Chicago Union Railroad came directly through it. Within a couple of years, five hundred inhabitants were living there, some of them commuting to work in the city, and they were a sober, diligent bunch. Soon a school, the Illinois Institute, was under construction in their midst (Worster, p. 54).

In 1859, President Jonathan Blanchard of Knox College in Galesburg, Illinois, left there to become the institute's first leader. Early in his tenure, he proposed that the school be called Wheaton College, probably to encourage further generosity from the brothers who were its first benefactors. The school's vision was "a combination of intellectual growth and Christian faith"

(Wheaton College). Because Blanchard was an avid abolitionist, it's no surprise that the student body contributed some 67 soldiers to the Union cause during the Civil War.

Blanchard served Wheaton until 1882. Then, as was not unusual in those times, he was succeeded in the presidency by his son, Charles Albert, whose run was equally impressive—all the way to 1925. An 1870 alumnus of the college, he built both the curriculum and the campus. Science and the industrial arts became important parts of the college (Wheaton College).

One of the fortunate group of antebellum liberal arts institutions to survive and prosper during the successive waves of competition, Wheaton today is a member of the Consortium of Liberal Arts Colleges. The consortium is an organization "comprising many of the top liberal arts colleges in the United States, chartered to explore and promote the use of information technology in the service of [their] liberal arts educational missions" (Consortium of Liberal Arts Colleges). Dating to 1984 and naming as its founding catalyst President S. Frederick Starr of Oberlin College, the consortium is a fetal form of the consortia that must be fostered for some sectors of higher education to fulfill its promise and its potential in the 21st century (see Worster, chapter two).

In the mid-1850s, the young Powell was drawn neither to Wheaton nor to the mother of all great Midwestern liberal arts colleges, Oberlin, though he briefly sampled both. Seeking science, he was drawn to Illinois College in Jacksonville. Founded in 1829 by the self-styled "Yale Band" of that university's alumni, Illinois College followed Yale University's example and opened a scientific department in 1852 (Worster, pp. 70–71).

Like Wheaton, Illinois College is among those early liberal institutions of the first wave that have survived into the 21st century. Today, one of nine Phi Beta Kappa members in the Land of Lincoln, Illinois College enrolls about 900 undergraduates. Among its 19th-century alumni was William Jennings Bryan, class of 1881. By its own account, "A basic strength of Illinois College is its large productive endowment" (Illinois College). Along with membership in a consortium, a large and productive endowment is a key to the survival of these precious morsels in the roiling stew of 21st-century American higher education.

When Powell, after the Civil War, commenced his career as a western explorer and scientist, among his first patrons he counted the new Illinois Industrial University, now the University of Illinois. Here, at last, having had three years of college education by moving among Wheaton, Oberlin, and Illinois College, Powell encountered an early arrival on the second great wave of American higher education.

Ever since the first student walked through its doors in 1867, the University of Illinois has been a tremendous resource for the State of Illinois. Founded in response to the federal Land Grant Act of 1862, the University immediately met an important need to provide higher education opportunities for working class people (University of Illinois).

Today, the University of Illinois employee more than 6,000 faculty, 6,500 administrators and other professionals, and 8,700 graduate assistants. It awards approximately 20,500 degrees per year and counts more than half a million living alumni. Its annual operating budget is about $5.64 billion, while it enrolls some 78,500 students in 800 buildings scattered across three campuses (University of Illinois).

The Third Wave: 1900–1945

While one might choose any of the great private universities to illustrate the third great wave in American higher education, I have selected Case Western Reserve University for two reasons. The first reason is personal: Case Western Reserve is my alma mater; I care about it very much and come to this place in my narrative knowing something about it. The second is that Case Western Reserve—today one of the 30-plus American universities in the so-called "Billion Dollar Club," comprising institutions boasting $1 billion or more of endowment—is a splendid example of a resilient institution, whose long history spans all four great waves identified above and which seems well positioned to survive and prosper in this fifth one.

Western Reserve Academy, founded in Hudson, Ohio, in 1826, can be counted among the proliferation of liberal arts colleges established during the first wave. Of the 800 such colleges founded during that 85-year cycle, only about 180 survived the second great wave of land-grant institutions during the second half of the 19th century. In 1880, the college moved to Cleveland. Amasa Stone, an ally of Vanderbilt and an adversary of Rockefeller, financed the move. Said to be the "richest man in Cleveland," he gave the college $600,000 over a three-year period (Cramer, pp. 77–78).

In 1881, the Case School of Applied Science opened in downtown Cleveland. Through the sustained generosity and vision of Stone and other moneyed Clevelanders, 43 acres were acquired on Cleveland's east side, and Case's first permanent building was built beside the new facilities of Western Reserve. Thus, Western Reserve University and Case Institute of Technology, as the institutions came to be named, grew together, their campuses more or less divided by Euclid Avenue, the city's major east–west thoroughfare. Symbolic of the symbiosis between the two institutions was the Michelson–Morley ether-drift experiment in 1887. Albert Michelson was a Case physicist who was at The University of Chicago by the time he won a Nobel Prize for his work. Edward Morley was a Western Reserve chemist. Their collaboration would one day help confirm Einstein's theoretical work (Cramer, pp. 57–70).

While the two institutions would not formally merge until 1967, in a very real sense they were to Cleveland what The University of Chicago was to the Windy City and Carnegie Mellon University was to Pittsburgh for the half century before they tied the legal knot.

It was the titans of the American industry, enriched, sometimes to fabulous levels of wealth, during the latter half of the 19th century, who built these great private universities. Case in point was Rockefeller. No industrial magnate's story is more closely tied to the rise of American industrial might than his. On February 1, 1865, Rockefeller bid $72,500 and bought his first oil refinery—in Cleveland. "I ever point to that day as the beginning of the success I have made of my life," he later wrote (Yergin, p. 35). The purchase was the start of the rationalization of the chaos that was the western Pennsylvania oil boom. And Standard Oil was the instrument of Rockefeller's power. By the end of the 1870s, Rockefeller and his associates ruled an empire of refineries, pipelines, and oil fields that amounted to a near monopoly.

So powerful had Standard Oil become by the turn of the century that in 1904, recently re-elected President Theodore Roosevelt targeted the conglomerate for attack under the newly enacted Sherman Anti-Trust Act. In 1909, the federal district court found in favor of the government in its suit to bust the Standard Oil trust, and in 1911, the U.S. Supreme Court affirmed that verdict. Although the remedy resulted in the creation of seven separate companies from the Standard monopoly, the so-called Seven Sisters (Yergin, pp. 109–110), Rockefeller himself would end up even wealthier than before the lawsuit. Indeed, he was the wealthiest American of his time, his riches surpassed only by some few potentates and royal families.

Rockefeller's charitable activities touched a wide range of causes and projects. In higher education, his baby was The University of Chicago, where his largess enabled the theft of top faculty from competitor institutions around the nation, including Michelson of Case (Cramer, p. 213). But Rockefeller did not ignore the leading private institutions of his hometown. For example, in 1904, he provided Case with $200,000 to build two new buildings, one for physics, and the other dedicated to mining and metallurgy (Cramer, p. 243).

The Fourth Wave: 1945–2000

For a while, at least, all boats rose on the gargantuan fourth wave of American higher education. Millions of returning servicemen, supported by the GI Bill, sought learning at institutions of all shapes and sizes across the country. To this day, the odd Quonset hut, hastily erected to help house this vast influx, is still being used in one way or another on a few campuses. While World War II devastated the rest of the world, the United States was much more than just untouched: its economy was strengthened and expanded. Population growth drove a housing boom that swept into the countryside, where William Levitt used Henry Ford's techniques in the development of the suburban sprawl (Halberstam, p. 132).

Added to the influx of students was an influx of government funding as higher education was enlisted into the Cold War in the 1950s. The Vietnam War kept the largess flowing throughout the 1960s, notwithstanding the leftist critique of the megaversity and the antiwar sentiment and the campus violence the war spawned. Only in the 1970s, as the war wound down and new competition—notably, a proliferation of community colleges—grew did the quarter century of growth and affluence show signs of weakening.

By the early 1970s, many universities were overbuilt and financially overextended. The male student population dropped off as the military draft gave way to a lottery system and then ended entirely. In Cleveland, meanwhile, two new institutions, Cleveland State University and Cuyahoga Community College, competed primarily for undergraduates with Case Western Reserve and the other private colleges and universities in the city. On top of all this, in Cleveland, the great steel mills were starting to contract and finally close in the face of foreign competition from countries economically recovered from World War II. During the first year of its merger, Case Reserve suffered a $3 million deficit. Shortfalls of $4 million followed in each of the succeeding three fiscal/academic years (Cramer, p. 284).

During the past three decades, higher education has pursued a range of strategies that have enabled most of its institutions to survive challenges and even to grow and prosper. Numerous colleges have expanded their offerings and activities and become universities.

Major private institutions such as Case Western Reserve discovered the capital campaign, and learned to overlap the private stage of each new campaign with the public stage of the one just winding down, ideally having surpassed its stated monetary goal. By the end of the century, billion-dollar capital campaigns had become almost common. The billion-dollar club among university endowments at the turn of this century included some 30 members. Harvard is consistently on top with an endowment approaching $37-plus billion, and the likes of Case Western Reserve brought up the rear with about $1.5–2.0 billion in the bank (Chronicle of Higher Education).

Prestigious liberal arts institutions, some dating all the way back to the first wave—such as Swarthmore, Haverford, Bryn Mawr, and Franklin & Marshall colleges in Southeastern Pennsylvania—chose to remain small, selective colleges and enjoyed the financial soundness to sustain that choice (Chronicle of Higher Education).

Public universities, enduring declining appropriations, learned to play the endowment game, cultivating contributions from their often-vast alumni associations, while competing successfully for the soft dollars of government and private grants. Community colleges are also learning to raise private funds in the face of legislative austerity, though their alumni are not so easily tapped, because many go on to shift their affiliations to four-year institutions. Population growth in the last decade of the 20th century helped all these boats to rise.

The Fifth Wave: 2001–?

American higher education entered the 21st century with great advantages. The world respected it and wanted what it had to offer. World population was growing, many would say at an alarming rate. And only one person in every 100 on this planet had a college degree. In short, there was a massive market out there and American higher education had the product that most in that market wished to purchase.

It must be added, though, that not all current entrants in the market were destined to benefit proportionally from this unique opportunity. To the contrary, some were not destined even to survive. Only two years into the new century, four U.S. colleges had closed (Selingo, p. A10).

However, no one should be surprised to learn that the many weak sisters among the large family of U.S. institutions were planning and striving to survive and to improve their financial and competitive positions. The surprising news was that Harvard's then-new, and already controversial, president, Lawrence H. Summers, was arguing that the nation's richest and most prestigious institution needed "nothing less than a cultural revolution on campus" (Symonds). According to an article, Summers had concluded that "Harvard

College is failing to provide undergrads with the education they need in today's fast-changing global economy." He also wanted to place Harvard at the center of education reform in medicine and the life sciences, making Cambridge/Boston the Silicon Valley of biotechnology.

While a powerhouse like Harvard can pick and choose the paths it will take to ensure its primacy in the new era, most colleges and universities may be said to be reacting rather than leading. And much of this reaction has been to the challenge of the for-profit, often Internet-based, competitors. For many schools, meeting this challenge meant a leap (often, a leap of faith) into distance-learning ventures. Early results were decidedly mixed. Some, like Temple University, shut down their e-ventures after losing a bundle and took a step back from the distance-learning market. This corresponded with some disappointing results for business schools that bet heavily on e-commerce programs (Alexander) only to be fried in the great dot-com meltdown of 2000–2001 (Carr and Blumenstyk, p. A-39). But the online learning enterprises of at least some traditional, nonprofit universities appear to be prospering down to the present day in the rough-and-tumble world of distance learning.

As for the for-profit bogeymen themselves, consolidation and collapse became the order of the day during the Obama years. Geoffrey Cox was correct 17 years ago that "a new wave of institution building" is occurring "right before our eyes" (Cox, p. 14). For example, the University of Phoenix started with a class of only eight working adults in 1976. Today, it is the nation's largest for-profit university, under the umbrella of a publicly traded parent, the Apollo Group. At its peak, it boasted of some 70,000 part-time students attending classes at 100 physical locations across the country. Its sister, the University of Phoenix Online, which trades separately from the Apollo Group, counted more than 25,000 degree seekers in its virtual classrooms as it marked a 47 percent increase in revenues and an 11 percent climb in profits between 2000 and 2001 (Brenowitz, p. 22). But in the second decade of the new century, Phoenix stumbled and enrollments slipped… more on this later.

The response of many traditional nonprofit institutions to the challenge of these for-profit players was to forge partnerships across the gap. Some prime early examples included the following:

- Columbia's Fathom teamed with four for-profits, including Kaplan Colleges,[1] to offer online learning.
- As the University of Phoenix made a second attempt to be licensed by the State of New Jersey, it announced in 2001 a deal with New Jersey

City University to use the latter's library facilities, thus overcoming a major problem that had led to denial of its application several years earlier (Smith).
- Corporate universities, which tailored their offerings to the perceived needs of major corporations in partnership with nearby colleges and universities, had reportedly ballooned from 400 to 2,000 during the first dozen years or so of the new era. Some examples included Walt Disney World and Valencia Community College; the Bank of Montreal and Dalhousie University; Ford Motor Company and Mott Community College; and The Hartford Financial Services Group and the University of Connecticut (Meister, p. B-10).
- Faced with increasing student enrollments and the deferred maintenance of aging dormitories, some institutions, such as McNeese State University and the University of North Carolina at Pembroke, partnered with such private developers as University Housing Services to build new residence halls (Sausner, pp. 35–36). (This is another trend we will explore more closely a bit later.)

Other traditional nonprofits were looking to merge with one another rather than partner with the for-profit sector. At the very start of this century, The Chronicle of Higher Education reported that "a wave of collegiate mergers...appears to be picking up steam. Since November [2000] six mergers of higher-education institutions have been announced. At least three more are in the talking stages" (Van Der Werf, p. A-26). In 2000, 24 of the nation's 28 Jesuit colleges and universities formed JesuitNET to pool resources, mostly via distance education offerings (McMurtrie, p. A-45).

Lastly, it's worth noting that a few universities were moving beyond the well-established study-abroad models of international institutional relationships to form more intimate links. These links were aimed at enabling the American partner to deliver desired educational services to needy foreign institutions, the logistical, financial, and cultural hurdles notwithstanding. For example, early in 2002, Purdue University signed a contract with Afghanistan's minister of higher education at the height of the War on Terror, under which the Midwestern university would work closely with the new Afghan government in the rebuilding of the shattered Kabul University (Del Castillo).

And, so, we plunged headlong into the surf, as the Fifth Wave broke on our shores.

Note

1. In May 2017 Kaplan was purchased by Purdue in the first such acquisition of a for-profit chain of campuses by a public university…more on this later, too.

References

Alexander, D., "E-M.B.A. Just Another Dot-Com Casualty," *Philadelphia Inquirer*, October 1, 2001.
Arnone, M., "Fathom Adds Corporate Training to Its Distance-Education Offerings," *Chronicle of Higher Education*, February 8, 2002.
Braudel, F., *The Perspective of the World* (New York: Harper & Row, 1984).
Brenowitz, S., "Phoenix Rising," *Matrix Magazine*, September 2001, pp. 21–23.
Carr, S. and G. Blumenstyk, "The Bubble Bursts for Education Dot-Coms," *Chronicle of Higher Education*, June 30, 2000, p. A39.
Chronicle of Higher Education, "The Chronicle Almanac 2002–03," Chronicle of Higher Education, August 30, 2002.
Consortium of Liberal Arts Colleges, Charter, September 24, 2002, accessed at www.liberalarts.org
Cox, G. M., "Why I Left a University to Join an Internet Education Company," *Change*, November/December 2000, pp. 12–18.
Cramer, C. H., *Case Western Reserve: A History of the University, 1826–1976* (Boston: Little, Brown & Co, 1976).
Del Castillo, D., "Afghanistan Signs Pact with Purdue to Aid Kabul U," *Chronicle of Higher Education*, February 14, 2002.
Fischer, D. H., *The Great Wave: Price Revolutions and the Rhythm of History* (New York: Oxford University Press, 1996).
Halberstam, D., *The Fifties* (New York: Villard Books, 1993).
Illinois College, Historic Years, September 24, 2002, accessed at www.ic.edu/About/historic.htm
Kazin, A., Fear of the City. In A Sense of History: The Best Writing from American Heritage, edited by Byron Dobell (New York: American Heritage, 1985).
McMurtrie, B., "Jesuit Colleges Try to Bring Their Values to Online Education," *Chronicle of Higher Education*, May 12, 2000.
Meister, J. C., "The Brave New World of Corporate Education," *Chronicle of Higher Education*, February 9, 2001.
Sausner, R., "Building Out of the Crunch," *University Business*, February 2002, pp. 35–38.
Selingo, J., "New England Loses Its Edge in Higher Education," *Chronicle of Higher Education*, February 15, 2002.
Smith, E., University of Phoenix. Personal e-mail to author, September 28, 2001.
Symonds, W. C., "Larry Summers Has an Ambitious Agenda to Remake the Nation's Leading University. Can He Do It?" *Business Week Online*, 18 February. September 24, 2002, accessed at www.businessweek.com/magazine/content/02_07/b3770001.htm

University of Illinois, University Profile. September 24, 2002, accessed at www.uillinois.edu/university.

Van Der Werf, M., "More Colleges Are Seeing the Virtues of Merging," *Chronicle of Higher Education*, March 23, 2001.

Wheaton College, "General Information: History and Heritage," September 24, 2002, accessed at www.wheaton.edu/heritage.html

Worster, D., *A River Running West: The Life of John Wesley Powell* (New York: Oxford University Press, 2001).

Yergin, D., *The Prize: The Epic Quest for Oil, Money, and Power* (New York: Simon & Schuster, 1992).

· 2 ·

THE FIFTH WAVE

A Deeper Dive

Fast forward to the second decade of our new millennium and meet the voice of higher education's doom: Professor Clayton Christensen of the Harvard Business School. In March 2013, Dr. Christensen garnered headlines with his prediction that by 2028 (i.e., in a little more than another decade from now), 50 percent of all American colleges and universities will likely be facing bankruptcy (Castagnera, p. 7).

The professor's prognostication was prompted by the then-imminent closure of Saint Paul's College, a historically black school founded in 1888 in Lawrenceville (VA). In the three years since that closure, others have followed in its wake. During the first half of 2015 alone:

- *March 2015*: Two small, Southern liberal arts colleges—Virginia's all-female Sweetbriar College and Tennessee Temple University, a Christian liberal arts institution—announced their intent to close the gates (Bidwell).
- *April 2015*: The for-profit Corinthian Colleges, once one of America's largest chains, abruptly closed its remaining 28 campuses, leaving some 16,000 current students stranded (Zillman).
- *May 2015*: For-profit Education Management Corporation announced the closure of 15 out of 52 Art Institute locations (Zillman).

- May 2015: Career Education Corporation indicated its intent to terminate its 14 Sanford Brown College campuses (Zillman).

While somewhat startling, this short sampling might not seem cause for concern, considering that institutions of higher education number somewhere between 3,000 and 5,000, depending upon how inclusive one wants one's list to be. Nonetheless, these failures have led some leading prognosticators to join Clay Christensen in predicting an accelerating trend. Notably, in September 2015, Moody's Investor Service released a report that highlighted "a persistent inability among small colleges to increase revenues," with the resulting prediction that some 15 more such schools would close by the next year (Woodhouse).

Yet again, one might retort that these closures represent a miniscule percentage of the 2,300 private, nonprofit colleges that dot the American landscape (Woodhouse). The multimillion dollar question thus becomes: Is Dr. Christensen correct? Or, put another way: Are the current closures the crest of a coming deluge of institutional demises, or merely an extension of a steady-state historical tendency of a few colleges and universities to fail almost every year, since time out of mind? (See "Index….") An attempted answer to this question might begin with a summation of Dr. Christensen's "Disruption" theory.

The Innovator's Dilemma

In 1997, *The Innovator's Dilemma: When New Technologies Cause Great Firms to Fail* (Christensen) was a disruption in its own right. It quickly made Dr. Christensen one of the most influential business thinkers on the planet. *The Economist* anointed his book one of the half-dozen best of the 20th century's second half. Thinkers50 twice appointed him to a top ranking (Goldstein, p. B6).

In his introduction, Christensen says,

> This book is about the failure of companies to stay atop their industries when they confront certain types of market and technological change…. Such seemingly unaccountable failures happen in industries that move fast and in those that move slow; in those built on electronics technology and those built on chemical and mechanical technology; in manufacturing and service industries. (Christensen, p. 7)

His opening example is Sears Roebuck. He cites *Fortune* for the proposition that in 1964 "everybody in its organization simply did the right thing, easily and naturally. And their cumulative effect was to create a powerhouse of a company." But, continues Christensen in 1997,

> [N]o one speaks about Sears that way today. Somehow, it completely missed the advent of discount retailing and home centers. In the midst of today's catalogue retailing boom, Sears has been driven from that business. Indeed, the very viability of its retailing operations has been questioned. (Christensen, p. 7)

The Innovator's Dilemma is replete with additional examples of once-prosperous companies falling from grace in the face of cheaper competitors. Some 165 pages later, he offers a summation of his thesis in seven succinct points:

- "[T[he pace of progress that markets demand or can absorb may be different from the progress offered by technology." That, he claims, means that products apparently not useful to today's customers, i.e., disruptive technologies, may be just the ticket tomorrow.
- Managing innovation means giving enough resources to the right technologies and letting others starve.
- Then you need to match the market with the new technology.
- Most companies' capabilities are a lot more specialized than their managers realize.
- The information may not even exist to make large and decisive investments in new, disruptive technologies.
- Disruptive technologies favor "first movers."
- Bottom line, despite their technology, brands, manufacturing prowess, managerial experience, distribution clout, and cash on hand, successfull, established firms have a hard time flexing to innovations that don't immediately make money. "Because disruptive technologies rarely make sense during the years when investing in them is most important, conventional managerial wisdom at established firms constitutes an entry and mobility barrier that entrepreneurs and investors can bank on" (Christensen, pp. 173–174).

Application of this theory to higher education was but a short step for Christensen. The application of his thesis to higher education runs roughly like this: Higher education has never before faced a core technology capable of disrupting the status quo.

> [A]n Ivy League wannabe could follow only one route: intensive investment in facilities, faculty and the other indicia of a first-tier university. By contrast, Christensen

contends, today online learning is that missing core technology. Almost anyone now can capture, stream and distribute Ivy League-level content over the Internet. And this will blow the walls off traditional higher education. Put another way, why should a student borrow money, pay exorbitant tuition, and sit in a traditional classroom listening to a mediocre professor, when she can learn the same material from the top expert in the world in a MOOC (Massive Online Open-enrollment Course), for which her college will give her course credit? (Castagnera, p. 7)

Christensen spun out this higher ed adaptation to book length in *The Innovative University* (Christensen and Eyring).

In the past 20 years, Professor Christensen has become a cottage industry with two consulting companies guided by a son and a daughter, nine (mostly coauthored) books, and a reputed lecture fee north of $40,000 (Goldstein). At the same time, his disruption theory has come under attack, most notably by an in-depth examination of the 77 case studies in his seminal work. This paper reportedly finds that only 10 percent of the companies studied meet all the criteria laid down by Christensen (Goldstein). Meanwhile, the Harvard guru of disruption continues to expand his theory into such diverse arenas as religion and politics. And he holds fast to his prediction that, as online learning becomes more sophisticated and effective, it will be the disruptive technology that will put large swaths of colleges and universities under water (Goldstein).

Only time will tell if Clay Christensen is correct. But we should not wait another decade for the answer. Indeed, if he's right, that will be too late.

A Perfect Storm?

We should not wait because online learning is not the only disruptor of higher education crashing against the shores of our college campuses. Other forces also are at work, combining to create a potential perfect storm to disrupt the lethargic, the complacent, and the slothful among us. Those forces include:

- The decline of the middle class and, in particular, the erosion of home equity;
- Increasing competition among colleges and universities;
- The liberalization of credentialing, by which I mean the nearly universal ability of students to cobble together a college degree from a mix of life experiences, community college credits, AP examinations, as well as Christensen's vaunted online programs.

As in the book *The Perfect Storm*, these three "weather systems" are converging, such that Dr. Christensen's prediction may come true even though his theory of the cause is only a partial explanation.

The Middle Class and Its Diminished Home Equity

On December 14, 2014, *The Washington Post* explained "Why America's Middle Class Is Lost." Explained the article's author, "It used to be that when the U.S. economy grew, workers up and down the economic ladder saw their incomes increase, too. But over the past 25 years, the economy has grown 83 percent, after adjusting for inflation—and the typical family's income hasn't budged." Continues the piece, "In that time, corporate profits doubled as a share of the economy. Workers today produce nearly twice as many goods and services per hour on the job as they did in 1989, but as a group, they get less of the nation's economic pie" (Tankersley).

The New York Times agreed. "The middle class, if defined as households making between $35,000 and $100,000 a year, shrank in the final decades of the 20th century." That partly, said the writers, was a good thing: many Americans moved into the upper-middle class, sometimes called "the affluent." But, since 2000, "the middle class has been shrinking for a decidedly more alarming reason: Incomes have fallen" (Parlapiano et al.).

And in April of 2015, *Time Magazine* joined the chorus of media voices singing the dirge for the middle class. "Under the traditional economic model, which ranks all American families by their incomes and then analyzes those in the middle, the median income of the middle class increased only slightly, by between 2% and 8%, between 1989 and 2013." But, the article continues, "if you use a different economic model that takes into account demographic and sociological attributes, such as age, educational attainment, race, or ethnicity, the median income of the middle class has actually *decreased* by 16% during that same period…." (Edwards). *Time* based this assertion on a report released by the Federal Reserve Bank of St. Louis, entitled *The Middle Class May be Under More Pressure Than You Think* (Emmons and Noeth).

Last but not the least, let's look at what *Fortune Magazine* had to say. Its June 20, 2015 article offered up the following disturbing data:

- America's child-poverty level is the worst among developed countries, even worse than Greece and Eastern European nations.

- Median adult wealth, standing at $39,000, ranks 27th, behind such countries as Cyprus and Ireland.
- Per capita median U.S. income is $18,700, described as both "relatively low" and "unchanged since 2000."
- 14.5 percent of Americans—north of 40 million—live below the official poverty line, putting the U.S. behind Albania and Morocco.
- The U.S. suffers from the fourth highest income inequality in the world, trailing only Chile, Mexico and Turkey. (Coplan)

As troubling as these data may be, equally or more cautionary for higher education is the decline in Americans' home equity… typically the major repository of savings for most of us. In 2011, the Federal Reserve Bank of New York revealed that home equity across the country had declined by 60 percent since the onset of the Great Recession in 2008 (Yedinak). As recently as September 2015, 4.4 million properties remained "underwater," i.e., in a negative-equity situation (Gerrity).

Why do these dismal data matter to higher education? The answer should be obvious: American families' ability—and willingness—to borrow for college costs have been profoundly impacted.

The dimensions of student debt are astonishing. Some 40 million Americans owe an estimated $1.2 trillion in student-loan debt (Rayfield). The class of 2014 graduated with average "mortgages" on their diplomas of $28,950, up 2 percent from the previous year's graduating class (Institute). Ironically, these numbers may be a giving us a glance in our rear-view mirrors, rather than a vision of the future. While tuition and fees at four-year public universities have risen 40 percent in 10 years, 29 percent at two-year institutions, and 26 percent at nonprofit privates, student borrowing declined 6 percent in the academic year 2014–2015 and was 14 percent lower than in AY 2010–2011 (Camera).

This gap between college costs and consumers' willingness and/or ability to borrow must be closed somehow. And one way—the major way—is tuition discounting. In 2003, nonprofit private colleges and universities reported average tuition discount rates of around 37.9 percent. In 2014, that average had risen to 48 percent. The average freshman in 2014–2015 received an institutional grant worth 54.3 percent of tuition. Eighty-nine percent of all incoming freshmen received some sort of a discount (Woodhouse 2).

According to the National Association of College and University Business Officers, "While the economy has improved, many families are still struggling. In a lot of communities you're seeing, if not job losses, jobs that don't pay nearly as much as they did. There's an increased inability [of needy students to go to college] and an unwillingness to pay even if you did have the money" (Woodhouse 2).

This phenomenon means that tuition increases, by and large, are negated by deepening discounts. Net revenue is growing at an anemic 0.4 percent annually in the nonprofit private sector of higher education. It doesn't take a Clayton Christensen to understand that this is a formula for failure, if the trend continues. Indeed, most administrators get it and many "are trying to leverage other strategies to recruit students, like freezing tuition, expanding marketing efforts, or increasing selectivity" (Woodhouse 2).

What expectations can we hold out for these strategies?

"When Everybody Is Somebody…"

"When everyone is somebody, then no-one's anybody," cautioned Gilbert and Sullivan in "The Gondoliers." In his seminal work on prioritization in higher education, Robert Dickeson captured that thought this way:

- "First, institutions' own marketing efforts to induce students to enroll have driven the accretion of academic offerings for several years…. This pattern of outbidding the competition academically is both costly…as well as usually futile" (Dickeson, p. 16).
- "Most institutions are unrealistically striving to be all things to all people in their quest for students, reputation, and support rather than focusing their resources on the mission and programs that they can accomplish with distinction" (Dickeson, p. 15).
- And "it is clear that colleges and universities have been adding programs, services, equipment, buildings, and public relations efforts to achieve greater reputational prominence" (Dickeson, p. 6).

Increasing selectivity requires increasing amenities in a sort of "arms race" with the competition. From 2001 to 2011, the percentage of university budgets devoted to "student services" increased from 17 to 20 percent. Observed one expert, "Schools are all going after a fairly small pool of students who are high achieving and high income and able to pay much of their own way to college. They're trying to build more amenities—so you hear about the rock climbing walls and the lazy rivers" (Schoen).

The crucial question, of course, is whether the consistent growth of higher education from the tiny liberal arts colleges of the colonial days to the megaversities of today, which I chronicled in Chapter One, will continue, or has our industry peaked prefatory to a protracted decline. "So if the big picture is of persistent growth over the long haul, of increasing numbers of campuses, instructors, researchers, administrators, support staff, undergraduates, and graduate students, how can we speak today of an apparently sudden reversal into decline?" (Alexander). Here's how:

- The number of students enrolled in colleges has declined despite growth of the American population. A 2013 survey of admissions directors found that 60 percent had fallen short of their enrollment goals (Jaschik). More ominously, that year's 2-percent decline hit four-year colleges hardest (Perez-Pena).
- As pointed out above, those students attending college are spending less on tuition due to a declination in home equity with a concomitant reluctance to tap into what assets remain, a trend countered by ever-increasing tuition-discount rates.

And so, here is the challenge: In order to compete for a decreased pool of "customers," universities are investing in (often-extravagant) physical amenities and a dizzying menu of majors, minors, and certifications…to be all things to all students. At the same time, declining tuition revenue demands trimming unprofitable programs. A combination of investment and cost cutting must results in a net revenue balance, or preferably a net gain, if a tuition-driven institution is to survive.

But, even if this strategy is executed ably by school administrators, will this prove sufficient? Here, we return to this chapter's start.

Liberalized Credentialing

In discussing this, I am circling back to Christensen's disruption theory, but with an expanded conception of its application to higher education. Where Christensen focuses on his so-called "core technology" of online learning, I propose to include here a wide range of options now presented to students seeking to gain a college credential as efficiently and inexpensively as possible.

- Dr. Christensen, as we have seen, grounds his prediction of a 50 percent fallout from private higher education upon the disruption being caused by online learning. The Babson Survey Group's 12th annual survey of online learning reported slower growth in 2014 than in prior years.

The slowdown was driven by an 8.7 percent decline in online enrollments in the for-profit sector (Grade Level). However, "The fact that online learning still grew illustrates that its fundamental appeal—primarily in public four-year institutions and private non-profit four-year institutions, according to the report—remains quite strong. Today's big news that Arizona State University will offer its freshman year online for credit at a price that, at last, positions an online program from a public university as disruptive will only fuel that growth is my guess. Furthermore, according to the report, the proportion of academic leaders who say that online learning is critical to their institution's long-term strategy is at an all-time high of 70.8 percent, and those institutions reporting that it is not a critical part of their long-term strategy has dropped to a new low of 8.6 percent" (Horn).

- Community colleges were particularly favored by the Obama Administration (White House), as well as many state governments. One result of this favoritism was (and pretty much still is) growing pressure upon four-year institutions to articulate their curricula so as to accept every credit earned at the lower level. An outstanding example is NJ Transfer (NJ Transfer), about which *Inside Higher Ed* observed, "A New Jersey law signed by the governor Thursday offers an unusual approach to easing transfer of community college credits by requiring that, upon acceptance, an associate degree awarded by a county college must be fully transferable and count as two years toward a baccalaureate degree at any of the state's public institutions" (Redden). This approach is no longer "unusual." Whether mandated by law or not, four-year institutions would rather have half a loaf than have no student at all.
- A growing number of universities also are awarding credit for life experiences.

One proponent has identified five ways in which various institutions facilitate this shortcut to a degree:

- Challenge examinations, which include the College Level Examination Program ; the DSST Standardized Subject Tests; Excelsior College Credit by Exam;
- Academic portfolios;
- Corporate training programs;

- Professional licenses and certifications, such as FAA pilot, engineer and mechanic licenses, and the respiratory therapist certification; and
- Military training (GETEDUCATED).

The upshot is that while Professor Christensen's disruption theory may be wanting in itself, it is receiving plenty of help from other educational trends and economic forces, such that the Harvard superstar's reputation may be rescued and his personal empire continue to prosper, as his prognostications pertaining to the dismal future of American, and especially private, higher education are proven to be accurate.

At any rate, prudence demands that his prophesies be taken seriously, lest through our lethargy they become self-fulfilling.

References

Alexander, Bryan, "Has Higher Ed Peaked?" *Inside Higher Ed*, April 7, 2014, accessed at https://www.insidehighered.com/views/2014/04/07/essay-considers-whether-higher-education-us-has-peaked

Bidwell, Allie, "Two Private Liberal Arts Colleges Will Shut Down," *U.S. News & World Report*, March 3, 2015, accessed at http://www.usnews.com/news/articles/2015/03/03/declining-enrollments-financial-pressure-force-two-liberal-arts-colleges-to-close

Camera, Lauren, "College Costs Rise, But Student Borrowing Declines," *U.S. News & Word Repost*, November 4, 2015, accessed at http://www.usnews.com/news/blogs/data-mine/2015/11/04/college-costs-rise-but-student-borrowing-declines

Castagnera, James Ottavio, *Handbook for Student Law for Higher Education Administrators* (New York: Peter Lang, Revised Edition 2014).

Christensen, Clayton M., *The Innovator's Dilemma: When Technologies Cause Great Firms to Fail* (Boston, MA: Harvard Business School Press 1997), accessed at http://jhqedu.com:1042/upload/books/Book1010/20140311115729871.pdf

Christensen, Clayton M. and Henry J. Eyring, *The Innovative University: Changing the DNA of Higher Education from the Inside Out* (San Francisco, CA: Jossey Bass 2011).

Coplan, Jill Hamburg, "12 Signs America Is on the Decline," *Fortune Magazine*, July 20, 2015, accessed at http://fortune.com/2015/07/20/united-states-decline-statistics-economic/

Dickeson, Robert C., *Prioritizing Academic Programs and Services: Reallocating Resources to Achieve Strategic Balance* (San Francisco, CA: Jossey Bass, Revised Edition 2010).

Edwards, Haley Sweetland, "The Middle Class Is Doing Worse Than You Think," *Time Magazine*, April 8, 2015, accessed at http://time.com/3814048/income-inequality-middle-class/

Emmons, William R. and Bryan J. Noeth, *The Middle Class May Be Under More Pressure Than You Think* (Federal Reserve Bank of St. Louis 2015), accessed at https://www.stlouisfed.org/publications/in-the-balance/issue11-2015/the-middle-class-may-be-under-more-pressure-than-you-think

Gerrity, Michael, "4.4 Million U.S. Properties Remain in Negative Equity," *World Property Journal*, September 15, 2015, accessed at http://www.worldpropertyjournal.com/real-estate-news/united-states/irvine/negative-equity-housing-data-2015-frank-nothaft-corelogic-national-home-price-index-hpi-home-foreclosure-data-completed-foreclosures-frank-nothaft-anand-nallathambi-real-estate-news-9358.php

"5 Ways to Earn College Credit for Career and Life Experience," GETEDUCATED, accessed at http://www.geteducated.com/cutting-online-university-cost/145-online-life-experience-degree

Goldstein, Evan R., "The Undoing of Disruption," *The Chronicle Review*, October 2, 2015, pp. B6–B9.

Grade Level: Tracking Online Education in the United States, Online Learning Consortium (2015), accessed at http://onlinelearningconsortium.org/read/survey-reports-2014/

Horn, Michael, "Report That Says Online Learning Growth Is Slowing Misses Big Picture," *Forbes*, April 23, 2015, accessed at http://www.forbes.com/sites/michaelhorn/2015/04/23/report-that-says-online-learning-growth-is-slowing-misses-big-picture/

"Index of Colleges and Universities that Have Closed, Merged, or Changed Names," *College History Garden*, November 25, 2014, accessed at http://collegehistorygarden.blogspot.com/2014/11/index-of-colleges-and-universities-that.html

Institute for College Access & Success, *Student Debt and the Class of 2014*, October 2015, accessed at http://ticas.org/sites/default/files/pub_files/classof2014.pdf

Jaschik, Scott, "Feeling the Heat: The 2013 Survey of College and University Admissions Directors," *Inside Higher Ed*, September 18, 2013, accessed at https://www.insidehighered.com/news/survey/feeling-heat-2013-survey-college-and-university-admissions-directors

NJ Transfer, accessed at https://www.njtransfer.org/

Parlapiano, Alicia, Robert Gebeloff and Shan Carter, "The Shrinking American Middle Class," *The New York Times*, January 26, 2015, accessed at http://www.nytimes.com/interactive/2015/01/25/upshot/shrinking-middle-class.html?_r=0

Perez-Pena, Richard, "College Enrollment Falls as Economy Recovers," *The New York Times*, July 25, 2013, accessed at http://www.nytimes.com/2013/07/26/education/in-a-recovering-economy-a-decline-in-college-enrollment.html?pagewanted=all&_r=1

Rayfield, Nicholas, "National Student Loan Debt Reaches a Bonkers $1.2 Trillion," *USA Today*, April 8, 2015, accessed at http://college.usatoday.com/2015/04/08/national-student-loan-debt-reaches-a-bonkers-1-2-trillion/

Redden, Elizabeth, "Un-complicating Community College Transfer," *Inside Higher Ed*, September 14, 2007, accessed at https://www.insidehighered.com/news/2007/09/14/newjersey

Schoen, John W., "Why Does a College Degree Cost So Much?" CNBC, June 6, 2015, accessed at http://www.cnbc.com/2015/06/16/why-college-costs-are-so-high-and-rising.html

Tankersley, Jim, "Why America's Middle Class Is Lost," *The Washington Post*, December 14, 2014, accessed at http://www.washingtonpost.com/sf/business/2014/12/12/why-americas-middle-class-is-lost/

White House, "Building American Skills Through Community Colleges," October 8, 2015, accessed at https://www.whitehouse.gov/issues/education/higher-education/building-american-skills-through-community-colleges

Woodhouse, Kellie, "Closures to Triple," *Inside Higher Ed*, September 28, 2015, accessed at https://www.insidehighered.com/news/2015/09/28/moodys-predicts-college-closures-triple-2017

Woodhouse, Kellie, "Discounting Grows Again," *Inside Higher Ed*, August 25, 2015, accessed at https://www.insidehighered.com/news/2015/08/25/tuition-discounting-grows-private-colleges-and-universities

Yedinak, John, "Home Equity Declines More than 60% During Great Recession Says Fed Report," *Reverse Mortgage Daily*, February 13, 2011, accessed at http://reversemortgagedaily.com/2011/02/13/home-equity-declines-more-than-60-during-great-recession-says-fed-report/

Zillman, Claire, "After Corinthian, Two More For-Profit College Chains Announce Closings," *Fortune*, May 7, 2015, accessed at http://fortune.com/2015/05/07/corinthian-college-chain-closings/

· 3 ·

THE DECLINE AND PARTIAL RESURRECTION OF PUBLIC HIGHER EDUCATION

Not so very many years ago, I belonged to a loose-knit organization of higher-ed labor-relations professionals. Most were employed by unionized, public universities in the United States and Canada. We held our annual conference each October in Clearwater, Florida. They traveled from as far away as California and Alberta to compare notes and, often, to commiserate. All 50 to 75 annual conferees represented the management side in collective bargaining and contract administration. Much of the commiseration revolved around the faults of full-time faculty and their labor unions.

But not far behind this perennial complaint was another increasingly bitter grievance that could be (and often was) summed up as follows: "We used to be state supported. Then we were only state affiliated. And now we are only state located."

The point, of course, was the ever-diminished amounts of public funding being allocated by a growing number of state legislators to their public colleges and universities. According to one authoritative source, "[S]tates have reduced their support by anywhere from 14.8 percent to 69.4 percent between fiscal 1980 and fiscal 2011" (Mortenson). This source identified the biggest losers as follows:

- Colorado reduced its support for higher education by nearly 69.4 percent, from $10.52 (per $ 1000 of state income) in fiscal 1980 (and a peak of $13.85 in fiscal 1971) to $3.22 by fiscal 2011. At that rate of decline, Colorado appropriations would have reached zero in 2022. Projections using more recent data found that Colorado theoretically would hit zero as soon as 2019.
- South Carolina reduced its state investment effort in higher education by 66.8 percent, from $16.72 in fiscal 1980 (and a peak of $18.19 in fiscal 1975) to $5.54 by fiscal 2011. Extrapolating this trend, state funding for higher education in theory would reach zero in 2031.
- Rhode Island reduced state higher-education funding by 62.1 percent between 1980 and 2011, from $9.81 to $3.72. The state effort peaked at $10.35 in fiscal 1981. Extrapolating this trend, state funding for higher education would bottom out in 2031.
- Arizona reduced its annual state investment effort by 61.9 percent from $12.27 in fiscal 1980 to $4.68 by fiscal 2011. This effort had peaked earlier at $15.13 in fiscal 1974. The trend between 1980 and 2011 would have landed at zero in 2032, although more recent data indicated it could have been even sooner.
- Oregon reduced its state higher education investment by 61.5 percent, from $10.85 in fiscal 1980 (and $12.77 in fiscal 1970) to $4.18 in 2011. Extrapolating this trend since fiscal 1980, state investment would reach zero in 2036.
- Minnesota reduced its higher education investment by 55.8 percent, from $14.17 in fiscal 1980 (and a peak of $15.08 in fiscal 1978) to $6.27 by fiscal 2011. Extending the trend since 1980 into the future, state funding for higher education arguably zeroed out in 2037. But another extrapolation hit zero in 2032.
- Montana was scheduled to reach zero, based on extrapolated trends since 1980, in 2034. Montana reduced its support from $10.88 per $1,000 of state personal income in 1980 (and a peak of $12.13 in fiscal 1983), to $5.08 by fiscal 2011.
- Virginia reduced higher education funding by 53.6 percent from 10.47 in 1980 (and $11.37 in FY1979) to $4.86 in 2011. At that rate, state funding would have reached zero in 2038. Another more recent projection reached zero in 2032.

- Vermont reduced its investment by 51.3 percent from $7.78 in 1980 (and $10.88 in fiscal 1970) to $3.79 by fiscal 2011. Extending this trend, Vermont hit zero in fiscal 2032 (Mortenson).

The institutions themselves were not the only victims of these austerity measures. On one hand, declining revenues—particularly in the wake of the Great Recession, which resulted in a severely eroded tax base for many states and municipalities—was a major catalyst. But politics also figured into the starving of public education. Voters sent conservatives into the governors' mansions and legislative chambers of many states. These politicos arrived with fiscally conservative philosophies and real or perceived mandates to cut taxes and break unions. Thus, faculty labor organizations, the banes of my colleagues in the Academy for Academic Personnel Administrators in Clearwater, were likewise pinned to the bull's eye.

In the 'banner' year 2014, a significant number of jurisdictions, some historically liberal union strongholds, were enacting or on the cusp of enacting bills intended to curb public-employee unions, including those at public universities:

- Federal. Senate Bill 5811. Democratic Senator Rodney Tom introduced a bill that would mandate that wellness programs be a part of state employees' health plans starting on January 1, 2014. Senate Bill 5811 also would have removed health care from the issues that are subject to collective bargaining.
- Tennessee. A bill was introduced aimed at denying teachers the right to negotiate through collective bargaining with boards of education about working conditions.
- Wisconsin. Governor Scott Walker's law, 2011 Wisconsin Act 10 that essentially eliminates collective bargaining for public employees, also requires employees to pay half of their pension costs and at least 12 percent of health care costs. It repeals most bargaining rights currently held by public employees, makes it legal for public employees to refuse to make payments to unions, and requires unions to hold annual elections just to remain in existence.
- Ohio. Senate Bill 5, which would have abolished most collective bargaining rights for public workers, was enacted, but later repealed by voter referendum.
- Iowa. House Study Bill 117 aimed to take health insurance and layoff procedures from the items that must be negotiated under the state's collective bargaining laws for public employees.

- Michigan. Several bills were in the works, including:
    - House Bill 4205: This bill would repeal the state's prevailing wage law that requires union-scale pay for all public construction projects, and which establishes rates of pay based on collective bargaining.
    - SB 120: This bill would allow counties and local governments to create "right-to-work" zones, in which employers would be prohibited from requiring workers to be union members as a condition of employment.
    - House Bill 4205: This bill would repeal binding arbitration for police and firefighters. [http://www.csg.org/pubs/capitolideas/enews/issue66_2.aspx]
- Illinois. Governor Pat Quinn signed SB1556, a law that allows the governor to deny collective bargaining rights for up to 3,580 managers and supervisors. The law applies to managerial or supervisory positions under the governor and other statewide offices—such as the secretary of state and attorney general—that are not currently represented by a union or those who have gained representation since December 2008.
- Kansas. House Bill 2027 was intended to drastically reduce teachers' collective bargaining rights: The measure would reduce from 30 to five the number of issues that teachers could negotiate with local school boards. For example, teachers could still negotiate for pay and sick leave, but not performance evaluations. And opponents of the bill said even pay negotiations would be undermined because the legislation would allow an alternative pay plan for some teachers.
- Arizona. There were three bills passed that restrict organized labor in the state:
    - SB1348: Prohibits public employers from paying a public employee for any union activity, although employees are still able to receive compensated leave for personal reasons.
    - SB1349: Public employers are prohibited from deducting any payments to a third party from an employee's paycheck unless the employee provides annual written or electronic permission.
    - SB1350: Prohibits those providing contracted labor or services to the state or a political subdivision, such as a city or town, from striking or stopping work in any other way (Filipp and Castagnera).

Regarding the reductions in direct funding to public universities, colleges and community colleges, the slack was taken up by increased tuition and fees, as well as (in many instances, very ambitious) fund-raising initiatives. Although ostensibly founded to serve the citizens of their home states, many of these schools initiated vigorous out-of-state and even international recruiting efforts. Tuition and fees, which were declining back in the 1970s, ballooned, especially at flagship state systems. "Inflation-adjusted tuition charges that were declining in the 1970s have surged since 1980. Inflation-adjusted tuition and fee charges have increased by 247 percent at state flagship universities, by 230 percent at state universities and colleges, and by 164 percent at community colleges since 1980" (Mortenson). While financially capable out-of-state students typically coughed up three times the in-state tuition rates for such schools, poorer state residents increasingly found their home campuses economically off limits.

Some state-university initiatives, reaching beyond home-state borders, have been quite ambitious, if not to say dramatic. Herewith a few examples:

- "It's been four years since Harvard Business School's Clayton Christensen, the father of disruptive innovation theory, warned that technology would bring large-scale change to higher education. Universities have since been rolling out hundreds of online degree programs and thousands of free massive open online courses. But one of the most potentially disruptive initiatives in education launched on Wednesday at Arizona State University and edX, the online learning nonprofit founded by Harvard University and the Massachusetts Institute of Technology. Arizona State will allow students anywhere in the world to take their entire freshman year of courses online and then use the college credit earned to complete undergraduate studies at either its campus or any other university willing to accept those transfer credits" (Byrne).
- "A $4 billion fundraising campaign unveiled last week at Texas A&M University ranks as one of the largest ever, as top public schools try to offset declining state and federal funding and stay competitive with private counterparts with longer track records of tapping donations. Texas A&M trails only the University of California Los Angeles, which is seeking $4.2 billion, and matches a drive at the University of Michigan, according to the Council for Advancement and Support of Education, a membership organization in Washington" (Bloomberg).

Case Study: New Jersey

While such dramatic initiatives proceed apace, state support for public universities is experiencing a comeback as this book goes to press in 2017, at least in some significant markets, as rebounding real estate values raise revenue boats. Consider New Jersey. While its neighbor across the Delaware River, Pennsylvania, is rich in private, nonprofit colleges and universities (the Association of Independent Colleges lists 89 Keystone State members), the Garden State is home to a mere 14 private colleges and universities; Princeton University being in a class by itself, the other 13 include:

- Bloomfield College
- Caldwell University
- Centenary College
- College of Saint Elizabeth
- Drew University
- Farleigh Dickinson University
- Felician University
- Georgian Court University
- Monmouth University
- Rider University
- Saint Peter's University
- Seton Hall University
- Stevens Institute of Technology

Most of the so-called "universities" on this list were mere "colleges" only a decade or two ago at most. By adding a few master's degrees to their menus, they qualified for "university" status, though their size and financial prowess in most instances was altered only marginally. From Caldwell to Felician to Georgian Court to Rider, they remain colleges in scale. And many are struggling with enrollment declines and operating deficits, to wit:

- *College of Saint Elizabeth.* "Some of the state's smallest colleges have been the hardest hit. The College of Saint Elizabeth, a Catholic college in Morristown, saw its enrollment drop nearly 35 percent between 2009 and 2014, according to data compiled by the state Office of the Secretary of Higher Education" (Heyboer).

- *Drew University*. For Fall 2016, this north New Jersey liberal arts college aimed for 385 freshmen, but brought in only 350, despite an average tuition discount of 58 percent (Hoover and Lika).
- *Rider University*. "Freshman enrollment was down—again. Only 865 new students had registered for classes, nearly 150 less freshmen than the previous year. Rider's total enrollment had been falling since 2009 and there were few signs the numbers would improve" (Heyboer).
- *Others*. "The declines were similar at Georgian Court University (down 24 percent), Centenary College (down 21 percent), Drew University (down 21 percent), …and most of the small and mid-size private colleges, according to the data" (Heyboer).

The declination wasn't uniform. Predictably, Princeton, New Jersey's representative in the Ivy League, posted enrollment growth in Fall 2015. So did Stevens Tech and Saint Peter's. Monmouth and Farleigh Dickinson held onto their enrollments, but only by the skin of their teeth (Heyboer).

Meanwhile, what was happening in New Jersey's much larger and more robust public sector? Let's see:

- *Montclair State University*. In February 2013, this northern New Jersey public university released it 2013–2017 *Capital Master Plan*. The plan opens with a look back at the previous decade: "Over the past decade, the University has allocated its resources in accordance with its strategic plan, focusing on faculty, facilities, student support services, and up-to-date technologies in support of teaching and learning. Underlying these priorities is enrollment growth of 36% from 13,502 students in fall 2000 to 18,382 in fall 2012. During this period, MSU dramatically increased academic space by 73%, adding 564,000 square feet for a total of 1.3 million square feet today. Despite this progress, Montclair State still has a conservatively estimated space deficit of 600,000 square feet when compared to similar institutions nationally" (Montclair). Thanks to a $1.3 billion higher education capital improvements package passed by the state legislature that year, the university was not long in closing that perceived "space deficit."

    "Montclair State University is poised to receive almost $94 million in State of New Jersey bond funding to expand its research and academic facilities and to upgrade its technology infrastructure when the Legislature approves the $1.3 billion higher education capital improvements package.

"The University's Center for Environmental and Life Sciences and the new School of Business building are two of the 176 shovel-ready projects proposed for legislative approval by Governor Chris Christie and New Jersey State Secretary of Higher Education Rochelle Hendricks. The Building Our Future Bond Act—which voters approved in November 2012—marks the first time in 25 years that the state has provided funding for capital improvements at New Jersey colleges and universities.

"The two buildings at Montclair State will support growing academic and research needs in the areas of science and business. The $55-million 100,000-square-foot Center for Environmental and Life Sciences will expand the University's science research infrastructure by 50 percent. The new facility will include teaching and research laboratories for the environmental and life sciences, a microscopy suite, and space to accommodate research partnerships with collaborating businesses" (State).

- *Rowan University.* The former Glassboro State University in the Garden State's agricultural south was best known as the site of a summit between President Lyndon Johnson and his Soviet counterpart back in the sixties…that is until an industrialist/philanthropist named Henry Rowan donated $100 million for an engineering school in return for the institution's name change in 1992. In the succeeding two and a half decades, Rowan has a medical school, a technology park, and a school of bioscience, just to name the major expansions (Rowan Gift). A $63 million business school building was ready for a "beam signing" in January 2016 (Beam-signing). Rowan has steadily increased enrollment to a total of 15,000 students in 2014–2015 (Rodia) and set a goal of nearly double that for the succeeding few years.
- *The College of New Jersey.* Like Rowan University, TCNJ traces itself back to less pretentious days as Trenton State College. The name change signifies more than an aspiration. With it came a dramatic upturn in its admissions requirements. Located in central New Jersey's Mercer County, TCNJ's ever-improving physical plant and academic reputation, together with its low tuition, regularly grabs the best and the brightest. The climax of this steady ascendancy climaxed in 2011 with the announcement of TCNJ's so-called "Campus Town."

"Utilizing the public-private partnership provision contained in the New Jersey Economic Stimulus Act of 2009, the Campus Town project will include the development of 14 acres of property adjacent to TCNJ's Ewing campus along Pennington Road. It will create nearly 300,000 square feet of housing and amenities, including 216,000 square feet of living quarters with the capacity to house 350 to 400 students....

"In addition to augmenting and enhancing the living–learning environment TCNJ provides for students, Campus Town will deliver amenities that will appeal to the broader Ewing community, such as retail stores, health and wellness facilities, and restaurants. Campus Town is envisioned to be a sustainable, walk-able, and environmentally responsible complex near the campus that will be an alternative to traveling by car to shopping and services along nearby Route 1....

"Slated for completion in the fall of 2013, the project is estimated to require an investment of roughly $50 million. The PRC Group, a multifaceted regional real estate owner, developer, and services provider, will assume all financial obligations associated with the project, and lead the development of the land. The PRC Group will also handle property management, with the support of residential and retail specialists unaffiliated with TCNJ housing programs. In addition, the West Long Branch-based company will provide TCNJ annual rent in a ground lease term of up to 50 years" (College of New Jersey).

This New Jersey case study is not being paralleled in all 50 American jurisdictions. As the Pennsylvania *contre temp* suggests, the impact of the public sector upon the private will vary along a spectrum. However, I believe some generalizations can be made:

- "That which does not kill us makes us stronger." (Nietzsche or "Conan the Barbarian," take your choice.)—Public universities, faced with the declination in state funding noted at the start of this chapter, were forced to adapt. Out-of-state recruiting, especially via online learning, as well as aggressive fund raising, helped the publics to weather the funding drought. Many universities and systems have become quite adept at these two tactics and will continue to use them to the detriment of private rivals for the indefinite future.
- Meanwhile, as with the New Jersey bond fund, many states have reinvigorated their support for their public colleges and universities.

- While the state-appropriations drought forced tuition and fee increases, the publics still enjoy a distinct cost advantage over their private rivals, notwithstanding 50+ % discount rates at many of the latter institutions.
- And, lastly, the aggressive attacks on public-employee unions and collective bargaining rights of faculties and other public-university employees will redound to the benefit of the publics in terms of cost containment in our still labor-intensive industry.

These four factors in combination ensure that the public sector of American higher education is poised to prosper and grow, not entirely, but to a large extent to the detriment of the private, nonprofits. Although in Fall 2016, nearly 30 percent of public universities missed their enrollment goals (Hoover and Lipka), the New Jersey example illustrates how rapidly ground can be regained and new markets conquered, when the state legislature exhibits a serious interest in that goal.

One final note: In mid-2017, the Illinois legislature passed its first budget bill in two and a half years. The public colleges and universities of the Land of Lincoln—arguably the most cash starved in the nation—finally got a little relief. Even they may be bouncing back from the brink.

References

"Beam-Signing Ceremony to Mark Milestone in Construction of New Rohrer College of Business Building," Rowan University, December 22, 2015, accessed at http://today.rowan.edu/home/news/2015/12/22/beam-signing-ceremony-mark-milestone-construction-new-rohrer-college-business

Bloomberg News, "Public Colleges Lift Bar on Fundraising Campaigns," *Indianapolis Business Journal*, November 12, 2015, accessed at http://www.ibj.com/articles/55750-public-colleges-lift-the-bar-on-fundraising-campaigns

Byrne, John A., "Arizona States, edX to Offer Entire Freshman Year of College Online," *Fortune*, April 22, 2015, accessed at http://fortune.com/2015/04/22/arizona-state-edx-moocs-online-education/

College of New Jersey News, "The College of New Jersey Announces 'Campus Town' Is Moving Forward," September 22, 2011, accessed at http://news.tcnj.edu/2011/09/22/the-college-of-new-jersey-announces-campus-town-is-moving-forward/

Filipp, Mark R. and James Ottavio Castagnera, *Employment Law Answer Book* (New York: Wolters Kluwer, 8th edition, 2013), pp. 10–34.

Heyboer, Kelly, "Why Is Enrollment Falling at Rider and Other N.J. Private Colleges?" NJ.com, November 8, 2015, accessed at http://www.nj.com/education/2015/11/why_is_enrollment_plummeting_at_some_nj_private_co.html

Hoover, Eric and Sara Lipka, "Enrollment Goals Remain Elusive for Small Colleges," *Chronicle of Higher Education*, December 11, 2016, accessed at http://www.chronicle.com/article/Enrollment-Goals-Remain/238624

Montclair University, *Capital Master Plan: Fiscal Years 2013–2017*, February 2013, accessed at https://www.montclair.edu/media/montclairedu/facilities/Capital_Master_Plan.pdf

Mortenson, Thomas G., "State Funding: A Race to the Bottom," American Council on Education, Winter 2012, accessed at http://www.acenet.edu/the-presidency/columns-and-features/Pages/state-funding-a-race-to-the-bottom.aspx

Rodia, Lauren, "South Jersey State Colleges Hit Record High Enrollment," *South Jersey Times*, September 22, 2014, accessed at http://today.rowan.edu/home/news/2014/09/23/south-jersey-state-colleges-hit-record-high-enrollment

Rowan Gift, The, Rowan University, accessed at http://www.rowan.edu/rowangift/story/

"State to Fund Nearly $94M for Capital Projects," Montclair State University, Spring 2013, accessed at https://www.montclair.edu/forward-thinking/spring-2013/state-fund-capital-projects/

· 4 ·

THE DECLINE AND CRIPPLING OF FOR-PROFIT HIGHER EDUCATION

Introduction

The fortunes of for-profit higher education rise and fall with the political tides. During the eight years of the Bush administration, this sector of the industry prospered.

In September 2004, as President George Bush's reelection campaign shifted into high gear, the Chronicle of Higher Education reported that his plans for higher education in his anticipated second term included "relax-[ing] certain rules that for-profit colleges must follow to participate in the federal student-aid programs." The September 7th article added, "According to a document released by the president's re-election campaign late Thursday night, Mr. Bush's higher-education proposals for a second term focus on eliminating restrictions that prevent adult and part-time students from receiving federal grants and loans" (Burd).

Four years, one Great Recession, and one historic substitution of a black Democrat for a WASP Republican in the White House, and a sea change in federal policy was in the offing. Two tidal forces surged out of Washington to whipsaw the for-profit side of our industry simultaneously. The first of these powerful political forces was a new set of proposed regulations from the Department of Education (DOE), aimed at punishing for-profit education providers, who fell short of their statutory mandate of graduating students qualified for "gainful employment." By the time the sun set on the Obama presidency at the close of 2016, two major players in the for-profit sector of higher education—Corinthian Colleges and ITT—had closed their dozens of campuses and ceased doing business, the most prominent victims of the DOE's campaign to clean up this sector of the industry.

The surprise victory of Donald Trump in November is likely to inaugurate significant changes at the DOE. As this manuscript was being finalized in mid-2017, Mr. Trump had named a billionaire with a reputation for hostility toward public K–12 education as the Department's Secretary. Does this portend yet another reversal of fortune for the for-profit sector of higher education?

I begin with a look back at the Obama Administration's harsh handling of for-profit higher ed and then move to a consideration of what may lie ahead for the likes of the University of Phoenix in 2018 and beyond.

2008–2016: Hard Times for America's For-Profit Universities

In a July 23, 2010 press release announcing its proposed regulations, DOE Secretary Arne Duncan commented,

> While career colleges play a vital role in training our workforce to be globally competitive, some of them are saddling students with debt they cannot afford in exchange for degrees and certificates they cannot use. These schools—and their investors—benefit from billions of dollars in subsidies from taxpayers, and in return, taxpayers have a right to know that these programs are providing solid preparation for a job.

The press release noted, "To qualify for federal aid, the law requires that career colleges and training programs prepare students for gainful employment in recognized occupations." Under the proposed rules,

> The Department would define whether a program successfully prepared students for gainful employment using a two-part test: measuring the relationship between the debt students incur and their incomes after program completion; and measuring the rate at which all enrollees, regardless of completions, repay their loans on time.

The picture painted by the DOE press release of the results of this test wasn't pretty. "The median federal loan debt carried by students earning associate degrees at for-profit institutions in 2007–08 was $14,000—almost double the median debt for their peers at non-profit institutions." By way of contrast, "while 88 percent of recent borrowers from nonprofit institutions and 80 percent of borrowers from public institutions were able to pay down the balance of their students' loans in recent years, only 55 percent of borrowers attending for-profit institutions were able to pay off more than accrued interest" (US DOE I).

Duncan's points were well taken. Federal student-loan aid could legally account for up to 90 percent of a for-profit's gross revenues. And, although fewer than 10 percent of the estimated 19 million students enrolled in institutions of higher learning took courses from for-profit colleges, those schools accounted for 44 percent of all defaults on federal loans.

In other words, big exposure combined with a high default rate added up to one big reason for the Obama Administration's interest in regulating the for-profit sector. Or, as Arne Duncan perhaps somewhat understated it, "While proprietary schools have profited and prospered thanks to federal dollars, some of their students have not. This is a disservice to students and taxpayers...." The DOE's proposed remedies included increased transparency. If the agency had had its way, "on or after July 1, 2012, unless the program has a loan repayment rate of at least 45 percent and an annual loan payment that is at least 20 percent of the discretionary income or 8 percent of average annual revenue…", the institution must "include a prominent warning in its promotional literature, and all other materials, including those on its Web site, and in all admissions meetings with prospective students, that is designed to alert prospective students and currently enrolled students that they may have difficulty repaying loans for attending that program...." More onerous yet, programs failing to meet specified debt thresholds would be deemed ineligible for further federal student loans. These could include an annual loan repayment rate of at least 35 percent.

More unusual than the proposed regulations—and, therefore, maybe more of a signal of which direction the Obama administration was steering the ship of state—was the exercise undertaken by the Government Accountability Office (GAO). The GAO engaged in what entrepreneurs in the retail world call "shopping." In the convenience store industry, for example, companies employ professional shoppers, who make purchases at selected store locations, then report back to the firm's security department if the clerks fail to properly record the sales. In the GAO's case, "Undercover tests at 15 for-profit colleges found that 4 colleges encouraged fraudulent practices and that all 15 made deceptive or otherwise questionable statements to GAO's undercover applicants." The August 4, 2010 issue of GAO Highlights reported, "Four undercover applicants were encouraged by college personnel to falsify their financial aid forms to qualify for federal aid—for example, one admissions representative told an applicant to fraudulently remove $250,000 in savings" (Government Accountability Office).

On the same date Duncan pronounced on the proposed regulations, Gregory Kurtz, managing director of the GAO's Office of Forensic Audits and Special Investigations, testified about these findings before the Senate Committee on Health, Education, Labor and Pensions. One upshot of these revelations was a dramatic decline in the stock values of publicly traded for-profit companies.

One well-known firm to take a hit was the Washington Post Company. Best known for its iconic newspaper—made legendary by Woodward and Bernstein during the Watergate scandal—its cash cow in these days of dying daily newspapers was subsidiary Kaplan.[1] According to one source, writer Mark Basch at Jacksonville.com, "Kaplan accounted for $1.46 billion of Washington Post's $2.34 billion in revenue" in the first half of the 2016 calendar year. "Kaplan had an operating profit of $166.9 million, while the company as a whole had operating income of $266.2 million." Coming clean on August 17th, the Post ran a story by Nick Anderson in which it confessed, "Late Friday, the Education Department released data on student loan repayment rates that showed 28 percent of Kaplan University's former students are repaying the principal on their federal loans. That was lower than the 36 percent repayment rate posted by the for-profit sector overall...." The story continued, "In a statement, The Post Co. said that 'a significant number of Kaplan schools' could be at risk of new limits on financial aid." The reference was to the proposed DOE regulations (Mufson and Yang).

Why would the Washington Post Company come clean? One reason may have been a flurry of security class-action suits filed against other for-profit corporations in mid-August 2010, in the wake of the GAO's revelations and the DOE's proposed rulemaking. Suits were filed in federal district courts against Educational Management Corporation on August 11th; American Public Education on August 12th; Lincoln Educational Services on August 13th; Apollo Group (parent of giant University of Phoenix) on August 16th; and Corinthian Colleges on September 1st. According to Kevin M. LaCroix, Esquire, of OakBridge Insurance Services in Beachwood, Ohio—author of the blog "The D&O Diary" [www.dandodiary.com]—security class actions "is a big business." Such an avalanche of class actions happens "where in one sector everybody has the same problem." He noted that "the same law firms are driving all these litigations." And, indeed, a review of the complaints in three of the five actions—against Educational Management Corp, American Public Ed, Lincoln, and Apollo—revealed they were all signed by Attorney Kim Miller of Kahn Swick & Foti of Fifth Avenue in New York City and Attorney Lewis Kahn of that firm's Madisonville, Louisiana office. Each of the complaints—filed in federal courts in Pittsburgh (PA), West Virginia, New Jersey, and Phoenix (AZ), respectively—were also signed by local counsel (LaCroix).

The Corinthian suit was filed by the firm of Pomerantz Haudek Grossman & Gross in the federal court for central California. The lead firm's homepage asserted, "Kahn Swick & Foti represents victims of corporate wrongdoing. Consistent with our goal to lend a helping hand is our mission to only accept payment at the end of a case, only if we win. And win we do. We have recovered millions of dollars for victims of corporate greed" (www.ksfconsel.com). As La Croix noted, the allegations in the complaints were all much the same. The plaintiffs asserted that between specified recent timeframes, each of the defendants made "a series of false and misleading statements" in their public pronouncements—such as registration and proxy statements, other SEC filings, press releases, and the like—which induced investors to buy their stock, which subsequently declined in value. While emphasizing that he had "no idea of the merits" of the claims, La Croix observed that it's "not a pretty picture." On his blog, La Croix identified yet a sixth suit, "a separate class action lawsuit against Alta College, Inc. (parent of Westwood College)… on August 11, 2010 in the District of Colorado alleging violations of the Colorado Consumer Protection Act." Observing "it seems safe to predict that other publicly-traded for-profit education companies could also be hit with one of these suits," LaCroix singled out Apollo Group for special attention. He wrote,

> The name Apollo Group may be familiar to many readers, as the company was the target of a prior securities class action lawsuit that has achieved a certain amount of notoriety because it is one of the few securities cases that has actually gone to trial. The trial resulted in a plaintiffs' verdict, although the presiding judge later set the verdict aside in a response to a post-trial motion. More recently, the Ninth Circuit (Court of Appeals) reversed the trial court's ruling and remanded the case to the district court for further proceedings, a development that has sparked significant interest and discussion. (La Croix)

When I interviewed him for a magazine article, LaCroix added that Apollo Group's "management disclosure practice has drawn a lot of attention." In fact, interest had long been drawn to the case of *Hendow v. University of Phoenix*

(Castagnera). In this case, Hendow and another former Phoenix employee claimed that the company illegally rewarded admissions officers on the basis of the number of students each enrolled. The case initially was dismissed by the federal trial court, only to be reinstated by the Ninth Circuit, which said,

> This case involves allegations under the False Claims Act that the University of Phoenix…knowingly made false promises…in order to become eligible to receive Title IV funds. Appellants, Mary Hendow and Julie Albertson (relators), two former enrollment counselors at the University, allege that the University falsely certifies each year that it is in compliance with the incentive compensation ban while intentionally and knowingly violating that requirement. (Hendow)

After the Ninth Circuit reinstated the case, the suit was finally set down for trial in March of 2009. Before the case could come to trial, the university's parent corporation, the publicly traded Apollo Group, settled with the government for $78.5 million, while also paying the relators' lawyers $11 million in attorney fees, according to published reports (Rubenstein).

Little wonder, in light of this news, one commentator on the Daily Show's blog (http://forums.thedailyshow.com) once ranted,

> It is crazy how the matchbook schools now market themselves as "universities." Many are basically predators on Title IV and GI Bill funds—basically taking taxpayer money and delivering content and certificates of dubious value…. The problem ones seduce low-income and freshly discharged military with unsupportable fantasies just to get their one precious opportunity to use public funding to better themselves. Instead they get crap.

While with regard to the for-profit sector as a whole, these allegations may have been unfair, it appeared that all publicly traded players might end up being painted with the same broad brush strokes to the detriment of their stock values, as well as their reputations. In April 2012, Apollo Group settled a stockholder class action initiated by a major public-employee pension fund for $145 million[2] (Gonzales).

The DOE's first run at imposing a "gainful employment" mandate fell flat, stymied by an adverse court decision (Duncan I). But the Department persisted and the second time was the charm, as the court challenge by the for-profit sector was rebuffed by the federal courts (Duncan II).

Even before the federal courts had finished with approving the DOE's second try at gainful-employment regulations, the casualties were being counted, as the following case study demonstrates.

Case Study: Corinthian Colleges

Three or four years ago, Corinthian Colleges, Inc. was one of the biggest and most powerful players in the for-profit sector of higher education. But by mid-2014, its neck was in the U.S. DOE's noose. The DOE's Federal Student Aid (FSA) office had placed Corinthian Colleges Inc. on an increased level of financial oversight after the company failed to address concerns about its practices, including falsifying job placement data used in marketing claims to prospective students and allegations of altered grades and attendance.

"The Department's foremost interest is to protect students and make sure they are educated by institutions that operate in accordance with our standards," said U.S. Education Under Secretary Ted Mitchell. "We made the decision to increase oversight of Corinthian Colleges after careful consideration and as part of our obligations to protect hardworking taxpayers and students' futures" (US DOE II).

Corinthian was the parent company of the Everest Institute, Everest College, WyoTech and Heald brands, which enrolled 72,000 students nationwide, who received $1.4 billion in federal financial aid money annually. All of Corinthian's campuses were required to wait 21 days after submitting student enrollment data to draw down money in FSA. The Department remained in close contact with Corinthian executives to protect the interests of the students enrolled at its various campuses.

The FSA places higher education institutions on heightened financial oversight for a variety of reasons. The Department had requested data from Corinthian multiple times in the prior five months to address inconsistencies in the company's job placement claims for graduates, but Corinthian officials had not turned over the documents. Since January 2014, the Department had sent Corinthian five letters requesting data and other documentation required by law. The Department notified Corinthian of heightened monitoring on June 12, which the company acknowledged in a subsequent filing with the Securities and Exchange Commission (US DOE III).

On June 23, 2014, the Department announced that it was working with Corinthian on a plan to avoid an immediate closure of the career training program chain and prevent suddenly disrupting the education of 72,000 students and the jobs of 12,000 employees. The Department and Corinthian subsequently signed a memorandum of understanding that required the company to develop a plan to sell and teach-out programs across the country over the next six months, including hiring an independent monitor approved by the Department to oversee its finances and the sales process. In exchange, the Department agreed to immediately release $16 million in FSA for students currently enrolled at Corinthian campuses. Corinthian was required to provide enrollment documentation to back up the funding request (US DOE III).

"Students and their interests have been at the heart of every decision the Department has made regarding Corinthian," said U.S. Under Secretary of Education, Ted Mitchell.

> We will continue to closely monitor the teach-out or sale of Corinthian's campuses to ensure that students are able to finish their education without interruption and that employees experience minimal disruption to their lives. The Department is committed to ensuring all students receive a quality education that leads to a well-paying job and a strong future. (US DOE III)

Under the agreement, Corinthian was required to put teach-out plans in place for all schools, including those for sale. An independent monitor approved by the Department was named to review matters related to ongoing operations and have fulltime access to Corinthian's financial and operating records. In addition, Corinthian was permitted to continue enrolling new students, but required to reimburse any students who enrolled in a campus found to be ineligible for FSA through the Department's reviews and investigations (US DOE III).

As noted, the Department put Corinthian on heightened financial monitoring with a 21-day waiting period for federal funds on June 12, 2014, after Corinthian failed to comply with repeated requests to address ongoing concerns over the company's practices, including falsifying job placement data used in marketing claims to prospective students and allegations of altered grades and attendance.

As part of the agreement, heightened financial monitoring remained in effect and Corinthian agreed to turn over data that the Department had been requesting for the last five months to address inconsistencies in the company's job placement claims for graduates, as well as grade and attendance records. Meanwhile, inquiries by the Department and other federal agencies into Corinthian's practices would continue (US DOE III).

With the swiftness of the changing tides, by early July 2014, the DOE and Corinthian agreed to an operating plan that provided the company's 72,000 students at the company's career colleges a chance to complete their education and protected taxpayers' investment, while Corinthian worked to either sell or close its campuses across the country in the next six months. The plan called for an independent monitor who would oversee this process for all programs owned by Corinthian, including Everest, Heald, and Wyotech campuses. "We have accepted an operating plan for Corinthian Colleges Inc. that will protect students' futures and fulfill the Department's responsibilities to taxpayers moving forward," U.S. Education Under Secretary Ted Mitchell reiterated. "Ensuring that Corinthian students are served well remains our first and most important priority, and we will continue to work with Corinthian officials and the independent monitor on behalf of the best interests of students and taxpayers. In order to ensure that Corinthian can still provide classes for its current students, the Department has agreed to release $35 million in student aid to be used solely for education activities—all of which must be approved by the Department." Under the operating agreement, which was effective July 8th, Corinthian also agreed to the following:

- Corinthian's campuses would inform students of their options, and every campus would institute a plan so students could complete their programs without disruption, if they chose to do so. The operating plan would also immediately halt enrollment at schools that were operating under this teach-out provision and require additional notification and disclosures for campuses that were being sold.
- Corinthian would only use FSA funds for normal daily operations, including student refunds, payroll expenses (including retention arrangements), accounts payable, interest and related fees, and related professional fees. Corinthian would not use federal funding to pay dividends, legal settlements of lawsuits or investigations, or debt repayments. Additionally, bonuses, severance payments, raises, and retention agreements would be reported to the monitor and the Department at least two weeks prior to the creation of contractual obligations and were subject to the approval of the Department.
- Corinthian would hire an independent monitor—approved by the Department—who would have full and complete access to Corinthian personnel and budgets to ensure prudent financial management and see that taxpayer-funded FSA dollars were spent well. The monitor would also review teach-out plans and sales of schools, and ensure students had multiple ways to submit feedback and any complaints about the process.
- Corinthian would also make refunds available to students in a number of circumstances. Corinthian and the Department would work together with the assistance of the monitor to establish a reserve fund of at least $30 million for Corinthian to pay those refunds.

- Corinthian would turn over all enrollment and job placement data required by federal law—and overdue to the Department since January—by July 15, 2014 (US DOE IV).

By the middle of that fateful month, the DOE took additional steps to ensure Corinthian Colleges' students and the American taxpayer were protected by announcing that Skadden, Arps, Slate, Meagher & Flom LLP & Affiliates, under the leadership of former U.S. Attorney Patrick Fitzgerald, had been selected to take on the role of monitoring various aspects of the career college company.

Pursuant to the operating agreement reached earlier in the month with Corinthian, the Department had required that an independent monitor oversee Corinthian's actions moving forward as the company began to sell and wind down its campuses over the coming months, and Skadden, Arps was tapped.

"Mr. Fitzgerald and his team will play a critical role in making sure that the Department is provided with an accurate accounting of Corinthian's operations to ensure students are protected as well as protecting the integrity of taxpayers' investment," said U.S. Under Secretary Ted Mitchell.

> The monitor will strengthen our efforts to ensure prudent financial management while overseeing an orderly process for students to complete their education—rather than students being left in the lurch as a result of an abrupt closure. With every action we've taken, our priority has been, and will continue to be, to put the interest of students first. We are confident that today's announcement underscores that priority. (US DOE IV)

Fitzgerald was appointed U.S. Attorney for the Northern District of Illinois in 2001 by President George W. Bush. As U.S. Attorney, Fitzgerald led several high-profile investigations and prosecutions, including the convictions of two former Illinois Governors, George Ryan and Rod Blagojevich. Fitzgerald was also selected as Special Counsel to investigate the leaks in the Valerie Plame matter and tried the case of *United States v. Lewis "Scooter" Libby*. Skadden was selected by *The American Lawyer* as a finalist in its 2014 Litigation Department of the Year issue and was named "Investigations Firm of the Year" at the 2014 *Who's Who Legal Awards*.

As articulated in the operating agreement the Department signed with Corinthian Colleges, the monitor was given full and complete access to Corinthian personnel and budgets for the company, review of all sales processes, and power to ensure that teach-out plans, which allow students to complete their program, were followed. The monitor also confirmed that Corinthian was in compliance with the production of documents and reviewed Corinthian's rosters prior to their submission for the drawdown of Title IV Student Aid Funds and also reviewed campus eligibility. In addition, the monitor—which was fully funded by Corinthian—oversaw that students and Corinthian employees had multiple ways to submit feedback and complaints. The monitor reported solely to the Department and did so on a regular basis.

As part of the operating agreement, Corinthian agreed to make full refunds available to students in a number of circumstances. Corinthian and the Department also agreed to work together with the assistance of the monitor to establish a reserve fund of at least $30 million for Corinthian to pay those refunds. Corinthian was limited in using FSA funds to pay only for normal daily operations, and, as noted it could not use federal funding to pay dividends, legal settlements of lawsuits or investigations, debt repayments, or payments related to private student loans.

In addition, the Department continued its investigation of various Corinthian campuses and continued to do so throughout this process. Under the Higher Education Act, the Department is responsible for ensuring the effective administration and oversight of the approximately $150 billion in FSA that is disbursed each year to all Title IV institutions. Corinthian received approximately $1.4 billion a year in FSA. For several months, the Department had been looking into serious concerns about Corinthian's compliance with federal law. This included assessing issues that had been identified through investigations conducted by other federal, state, and local agencies.

The Department announced that it would "work closely with Mr. Fitzgerald and his team in the coming weeks and months, to ensure that students are protected and have the information they need to make informed decisions about their education" (US DOE V).

The following year, Arnie Duncan's other shoe dropped. In April 2015, the DOE confirmed cases of misrepresentation of job placement rates to current and prospective students in Corinthian's Heald College system. The Department found 947 misstated placement rates and informed the company it is being fined about $30 million.

Specifically, the Department determined that Heald College's inaccurate or incomplete disclosures were misleading to students; that they overstated the employment prospects of graduates of Heald's programs; and that current and prospective students of Heald could have relied upon that information as they were choosing whether to attend the school. Heald College had provided the Department and its accreditors this inaccurate information as well.

The Department also notified Corinthian it intended to deny Corinthian's pending applications to continue to participate in the Title IV FSA programs at its Heald Salinas and Stockton locations. Corinthian had 14 days to respond to the Department's notice, after which the Department would issue its final decision. Moreover, the Department determined that Heald College was no longer allowed to enroll students and must prepare to help its current students either complete their education or continue it elsewhere.

Commented the DOE's Press Office,

> The Obama Administration has led unprecedented efforts to protect consumers from predatory career colleges. It has established new gainful employment regulations to hold career-training programs accountable and ensure that students are not saddled with debt they cannot repay. These regulations ensure that programs improve their outcomes for students—or risk losing access to federal student aid. Last year, the Department announced a new federal interagency task force to help ensure proper oversight of for-profit institutions, which will be led by Under Secretary Ted Mitchell.

"This should be a wake-up call for consumers across the country about the abuses that can exist within the for-profit college sector," Secretary Arne Duncan said of the Department's enforcement action against Corinthian. "We will continue to hold the career college industry accountable and demand reform for the good of students and taxpayers. And we will need Congress to join us in that effort."

"Instead of providing clear and accurate information to help students choose which college to attend, Corinthian violated students' and taxpayers' trust," added Under Secretary Mitchell. He continued,

> Their substantial misrepresentations evidence a blatant disregard not just for professional standards, but for students' futures. This is unacceptable, and we are holding them accountable. As part of these ongoing efforts to ensure that career colleges prepare students for the workforce, institutions are required to provide accurate information about their graduates' job placement success and the types of employment their graduates obtained. The Department expects all institutions to adhere to the highest standard of care and diligence in following the requirements of participating in federal student aid programs to ensure colleges are always doing right by students and taxpayers.

The majority of Corinthian's campuses were sold to the nonprofit Zenith Education Group, which agreed to provide a number of new consumer protections, such as providing refund and withdrawal opportunities to students in poorly performing programs, and took steps to strengthen programs and improve affordability, including by reducing tuition. The sale allowed most students to continue pursuing their career goals without disruption, and the Department and the Consumer Financial Protection Bureau have since worked to provide more than $480 million in loan forgiveness for borrowers who took out Corinthian's high-cost private student loans.

In its investigation of Corinthian Colleges, the Department found numerous causes for concern with practices throughout the Heald College system. Some examples include:

- Heald paid temporary agencies to hire its graduates to work at temporary jobs on its own campuses—and counted these graduates as placed. For example, Heald paid companies to hire graduates for temporary positions as short as two days, asked them to perform tasks like moving computers and organizing cables, and then counted those graduates as "placed in field."
- Heald College counted placements that were clearly out of the student's field of study as in-field placements. For example, one campus classified a 2011 graduate of an Accounting program as employed in the field based upon a food service job she started at Taco Bell in June 2006. Another campus counted a 2011 Business Administration graduate as placed in the field based upon a seasonal clerk position she obtained in Macy's Shipping and Receiving Department during November 2010, which, the student stated, had ended prior to her graduation.
- Heald College failed to disclose that it counted as "placed" those graduates whose employment began prior to graduation, and in some cases even prior to the graduate's attendance at Heald. The Department's analysis revealed that, according to Corinthian's own data for 2012 graduates, more than one-third of the graduates reported to have been "placed in field" started their jobs prior to January 1, 2012, and over one-quarter started their jobs prior to January 1, 2011. And in follow-up interviews with some of those students, they told the Department that their jobs were not related to their fields of study, nor had they received promotions or increased responsibilities or otherwise progressed in those jobs because of their Heald education.
- In some of its disclosures, Heald failed to state that it had excluded students from its placement rate calculations, who the college said had deferred employment for one reason or another. In one case, a criminal

justice program claimed a placement rate of 100 percent, but it had classified almost 60 percent of the graduates as unavailable for employment. In another case, a medical-assistant program claimed a placement rate of 100 percent based upon 51 graduates having been placed, but it had classified almost 43 percent, or 38 of the 89 total graduates of the program, as unavailable for employment.

Throughout this process, the Department sought a wind down of Corinthian Colleges that protected students, safeguarded the investment taxpayers had made in their success, and created opportunities for students to finish what they started. In the following days, the Department provided more information to Corinthian's students to help answer questions about their FSA and their options. The Department also worked on a process to help federal student loan borrowers submit a defense to repayment of their federal student loans.

"We have kept students at the heart of every decision we have made about Corinthian, and we will continue to do so as we move forward," Under Secretary Mitchell claimed. "When our borrowers bring claims to us that their school committed fraud or other violations of state law against them, we will give them the relief that they are entitled to under federal law and regulations" (US DOE VI).

Two weeks later, Corinthian posted this announcement on its website:

Corinthian Announces Cessation of Effectively All Operations

All campuses closed effective Monday, April 27

SANTA ANA, Calif., April 26, 2015—Corinthian Colleges, Inc. (Nasdaq: COCO) today announced that the Company has ceased substantially all operations and discontinued instruction at its remaining 28 ground campuses. The company is working with other schools to provide continuing educational opportunities for its approximately 16,000 students. Corinthian said those efforts depend to a great degree on cooperation with partnering institutions and regulatory authorities.

Campuses closed include Corinthian's 13 remaining Everest and WyoTech campuses in California, Everest College Phoenix and Everest Online Tempe in Arizona, the Everest Institute in New York, and 150-year-old Heald College—including its 10 locations in California, one in Hawaii and one in Oregon.

Since signing an operating agreement with the U.S. Department of Education in July 2014, the Company has been focused on completing the orderly sale or wind-down of all of its schools. In November 2014, the Company announced that it had entered into an agreement to sell 56 Everest and WyoTech campuses to Zenith Education Group, Inc., a subsidiary of ECMC Group. As part of that sale, Zenith also agreed to conclude the teach-out process at 12 additional schools that were being closed. That transaction was completed in February of this year for all but three locations, the Everest College Phoenix campuses in Phoenix and Mesa, AZ, and Everest Institute in Rochester, NY. As a result of the sale, nearly forty thousand students were able to continue their studies and thousands of employees kept their jobs. Zenith has recently advised Corinthian that it will not consummate the purchase of Everest College Phoenix, and the closing conditions have not been satisfied for Everest Institute Rochester.

In parallel, the Company had been in advanced negotiations with several parties to both sell the 150-year-old Heald College and to arrange for teach-out partners to allow its Everest College and WyoTech students in California to continue their education. The Company said these efforts were unsuccessful largely as a result of federal and state regulators seeking to impose financial penalties and conditions on buyers and teach-out partners.

"We believe that we have attempted to do everything within our power to provide a quality education and an opportunity for a better future for our students," said Jack Massimino, Chief Executive Officer of Corinthian. "Unfortunately the current regulatory environment would not allow us to complete a transaction with several interested parties that would have allowed for a seamless transition for our students. I would like to thank our employees for their selfless dedication and commitment to fulfilling the educational and career goals of all of our students."

The Company said that its historic graduation rate and job placement rates compared favorably with community colleges. Corinthian also said that approximately 40 percent of its students previously attended a traditional higher education institution where their needs had not been met before attending a Corinthian school.

"Colleges like ours fill an important role in the broader education system and address a critical need that remains largely unmet by community colleges and other public sector schools," Massimino said. "Overall, our schools did a good job for the students they served. We made every effort to address regulators' concerns in good faith. Neither our Board of Directors, our management, our faculty, nor our students believe these schools deserved to be forced to close." (Corinthian)

And the Beat Went On

The speed with which Corinthian Colleges, Inc. was eviscerated by Uncle Sam (aka Arnie Duncan) puts its case in a class by itself. All the same, the company was not the lone casualty in 2014 and 2015. Other for-profit schools also drowned in the sea change that overtook this segment of the higher education industry in those two years. Here are some additional examples:

- Education Management Corporation announced the phase-out of 15 out of 52 campuses of its Art Institutes division. About 5,200 students attended the targeted campuses (Fain).

- Career Education Corporation unveiled a restructuring plan under which it would sell all its operations, except the Colorado Technical University and the American InterContinental University. The wind-up included the 14 locations of the Sanford Brown College and Institute, as well as the sale of its Briarcliffe College, Brooks Institute and Missouri College, which collectively enrolled 8,500 students (Fain).
- ITT Educational Services, operating 138 campuses enrolling 47,000 students, was simultaneously under investigation or the subject of suits in some 19 different states, the Securities and Exchange Commission, the Consumer Financial Protection Bureau, and the Justice Department (Cohen).
- In February 2015, Kaplan, Inc. sold all 38 of its Kaplan College Campuses (Fain).
- About the same time, DeVry University announced the closure of 14 campuses (Fain).

University of Phoenix the Ultimate Target?

The University of Phoenix, which dates its founding back to the 1970s, has long been the largest of the for-profit players in our industry. In 2001, I attended a two-week Harvard University program for midlevel university administrators. One of the leading guest lecturers on that year's syllabus was the CEO of parent Apollo. She challenged the student body, overwhelmingly from public and nonprofit institutions, to match her university's record of assessment. I detected an arrogance, a defiance of the prevalent, shared wisdom in traditional higher-ed circles that the for-profit arena was second rate. I think all of us in her audience had to admit to having our stereotypical views shaken, if not entirely changed.

By 2015, the University of Phoenix had pulled in its horns. Between 2010 and March 2015, its enrollment had shrunk from 475,000 to 213,800 (Smith). What's more, in October 2015, the Department of Defense barred U of P from recruiting students on military bases (Connolly). This banishment from military bases came after word that the Federal Trade Commission had launched an investigation of potential deceptive and unfair business practices. In the wake of the War on Terror, U of P reportedly raked in some $488 million in tuition and fees from returned veterans. The FTC demanded Apollo business records relating back all the way to 2011 (Samuels).

As noted earlier in this chapter, U of P has been on the bull's eye for decades. Former admissions counselors successfully accused it of illegal head hunting to build its student enrollments. It might not be unfair to say that in days of yore, for U of P and some of the other big players in the for-profit sector, fines for such misbehavior amounted to little more than a cost of doing business. But no more. As Secretary Arnie Duncan cautioned in late 2015, "The clock is ticking for bad actors in the career college industry to do right by students." (Samuels)

Before this DOE crackdown, some providers played the game pretty much like this:

- Recruiters enticed potential students, such as veterans, to enroll in their companies' educational programs, without much concern about either ability to pay or ability to perform academically.
- Students were assisted in obtaining federal aid, such as VA benefits and student loans.
- Those students—and their numbers were high—who washed out frequently defaulted on their loans.
- Meanwhile, the taxpayers' dollars had dropped to the companies' bottom lines, lining senior management's, owners', and shareholders' pockets, while Uncle Sam sucked up the losses.

Duncan and his Department determined to end such abuse. But by the end of 2015, Duncan's days in the DOE were numbered. And GOP presidential candidates, such as Senator Marco Rubio, were yet again touting for-profit higher education as the solution to whatever they claimed was wrong with the higher ed enterprise.

Meanwhile, in February 2016, Apollo Education Group, U of P's parent company, announced its decision to transition from a publicly traded corporation to a privately held firm. Its board revealed its decision to sell out to a group of private investors, led by the Vistria Group, for $1.1 billion. Former Deputy Secretary of the DOE Tony Miller, a partner in Vistria, was named as the privatized firm's Board Chairman-elect (Smith).

Apollo released the following public statement:

> Apollo Education Group, Inc. (NASDAQ: APOL) today announced it has entered into a definitive agreement to be acquired by a consortium of investors including The Vistria Group, LLC, funds affiliated with Apollo Global Management, LLC (NYSE: APO), and Najafi Companies for $9.50 per share in cash for both Class A and B shares. The purchase price represents a premium of 30 percent over Apollo Education Group's 30-day volume weighted average stock price for the period ended Feb. 5,

2016, and a 44 percent premium over the closing price on Jan. 8, 2016, immediately prior to the announcement that the Board of Directors was pursuing strategic alternatives. Tony Miller, Chief Operating Officer and Partner of The Vistria Group and former Deputy Secretary of the U.S. Department of Education, will become Chairman of the Apollo Education Group Board upon transaction close.

"The Apollo Education Group Board of Directors reviewed strategic alternatives and believes this transaction is in the best interest of all shareholders and strongly supports our transformation efforts," said Greg Cappelli, Chief Executive Officer of Apollo Education Group. "This new structure will allow Apollo Education Group the flexibility and runway it needs to complete the transformational plan at University of Phoenix, which will enable us to serve our students more effectively during a period of unprecedented volatility within our industry. We will also continue to expand our international operations and remain committed to driving principles of operating excellence."

"We are excited by the opportunity to build on the transformational work being done by the company," said Miller. "For too long and too often, the private education industry has been characterized by inadequate student outcomes, overly aggressive marketing practices, and poor compliance. This doesn't need to be the case. We are committed to accelerating and enhancing efforts to establish University of Phoenix as the leading provider of quality higher education for working adults and to continue supporting the organization's commitment to operating in a manner consistent with the highest ethical standards."

Miller was the Deputy Secretary and Chief Operating Officer at the U.S. Department of Education from 2009 to 2013. Miller oversaw day-to-day operations for a broad range of management, policy and program functions, spanning early childhood through post-secondary education. In addition to his operational responsibilities, Miller represented the U.S. Government at education and workforce development international forums and led the Department's missions to China, Korea, Japan, Singapore, Indonesia, Australia, New Zealand, Ecuador, Brazil, and Russia.

Upon completion of the transaction, Apollo Education Group will be privately held and its affiliated institutions will remain subject to the same U.S. and international regulations and accreditation standards.

The agreement was approved by Apollo Education Group's Board of Directors. The transaction is subject to financial, operational and customary closing conditions. It is also subject to regulatory conditions, including the expiration or termination of the applicable waiting period under the Hart-Scott-Rodino Antitrust Improvements Act, and approvals, including by the U.S. Department of Education, the Higher Learning Commission and state regulatory and programmatic accreditation bodies. In addition, it is subject to approval by a majority of Apollo Education Group Class A and B stockholders, voting as separate classes. Each of Apollo Education Group's Class B stockholders has entered into an agreement to vote in favor of the transaction. The acquisition is expected to be completed by Apollo Education Group's fiscal year-end, in August 2016. Apollo Education Group and Apollo Global Management are unaffiliated entities. (Apollo Education Group)

The rub was that the deal required DOE approval. On December 7, 2016 (the 75th anniversary of the Pearl Harbor attack, perhaps a bad omen), the DOE demanded that Apollo procure a $385 million letter of credit in order for the reorganized entity to qualify for Title IV funds (Korn).

Even before this demand was made, the deal was contingent upon a green light from Apollo's accrediting organization. Originally slated to close in August 2016, the close date moved to early 2017 in the wake of the letter-of-credit wrinkle. The DOE's decision was conveyed to Apollo's management in a letter that cited continuing enrollment declines that seemingly threatened the company's long-term financial viability (Korn).

Placing the decision in context, the *Wall Street Journal* observed, "The Department of Education has been cracking down on for-profit colleges in recent years and trying to ensure that hundreds of billions of dollars in student loans and grants are being used well, including requiring schools to post larger letters of credit as a safeguard in case of legal or regulatory troubles that cause closures. Chains including Corinthian Colleges and ITT Technical Institute have closed as a result of the increased regulation" (Korn).

Enter Donald Trump as the DOE Vice Tightened

When Donald Trump first threw his hat in the ring in 2015, pundits labeled his presidential bid just another chapter in a consummate showman's colorful career. When he began winning primary contests, these same pundits predicted his success was unsustainable. When, one-by-one, his opponents dropped out of the race, they said the GOP would rally behind one of the survivors, who would push Trump aside and secure the nomination. And, when Trump became the Republican presidential nominee, they said he could never prevail in the general election. His opponents, his critics, the pollsters, and the pundits were proven wrong every step of the way in the billionaire-entrepreneur's march to the White House.

Meanwhile, with far less fanfare, the DOE took a still more sweeping action. On Monday, December 12, 2016, U.S. Secretary of Education John King announced that his Department had denied the appeal of the Accrediting Council for Independent Colleges and Schools (ACICS).

Back in September '16, the DOE decided to strip the organization, which accredits some 250 for-profit colleges and universities, of its powers. The ACICS appealed. The denial of that appeal might seem to be its death knell.

If so, what will this mean for the for-profit sector of the higher ed industry? Quite simply, it could mean that the schools currently accredited by ACICS will no longer be qualified to partake of the $150 billion federal student grant-and-loan cornucopia. And, since—as we have seen—such federal funding is the lifeblood of most of these organizations, they could go bankrupt, as did two major for-profit players, Corinthian Colleges and ITT.

The ACICS came under fire two years ago, when it continued accreditation of Corinthian Colleges. At the time, despite having numerous campuses and thousands of students, Corinthian, as we have seen, was under investigation by some 20 federal and state entities regarding allegations of defrauding its students. When the DOE cut Corinthian off from the federal student-loan spigot, the company (as we saw in our case study, above) quickly collapsed, leaving thousands of active students scrambling to pay off loans and find berths at alternative institutions. Ultimately, the DOE provided many of them with relief, such as deferred-payment options.

Meanwhile, the National Advisory Committee on Institutional Quality and Integrity, reportedly at the instigation of the DOE, voted back in June 2016 to yank ACICS's accrediting authority. The DOE acted on that recommendation in the early fall. In denying the appeal, Secretary King cited "a profound lack of compliance with the most basic Title IV (student loan) responsibilities of a nationally recognized accreditor," such as assessing student achievement, determining licensure standards, and monitoring troubled schools.

For his part, ACICS Interim President Roger Williams decried the decision, warning it will "result in immediate and meaningful harm to hundreds of thousands of students currently enrolled in ACICS-accredited institutions" (Douglas-Gabriel).

Simultaneously, during November and December 2016, amidst the hand wringing, the second-guessing, the Monday-morning quarterbacking, and Green Party candidate Jill Stein's lawsuits, the president-elect proceeded to select his cabinet members. And given that the GOP controls the Congress, prudence permitted an assumption that his nominees would be confirmed. With rare exceptions[3] that assumption proved correct.

His choice for Secretary of Education was Betsy DeVos, described by a popular women's magazine as

> a billionaire businesswoman who chairs a company called the Windquest Group that invests in technology, manufacturing, and clean energy. Her nonprofit work is extensive, particularly in the field of education, where she's raised money for charter schools.

She's also a high-profile Republican fundraiser and held prominent roles in the Michigan Republican Party, including chairwoman from 1996 to 2000. (Sebastian)

The unions that represent public school teachers (chiefly the National Education Association and the American Federation of Teachers) reportedly were "furious" over the appointment, because DeVos has a track record as a vocal proponent of charter schools. They have branded her "ideological" and "anti-public education." Michigan ACLU Executive Director Kary Moss points to DeVos's efforts to steer funding from public schools to private and parochial alternatives. DeVos and her husband are said to have put their money where their mouths are, investing $1.5 million in an effort to block legislation intended to add oversight to charter schools in Michigan (Sebastian).

DeVos has no comparable track record on higher education. However, her commitment to the privatization of public K–12 education portends a preference for private, and especially for-profit, higher education providers.

Not all knowledgeable observers have shied away from their crystal balls, where DeVos is concerned. Dr. Pedro Noguero, distinguished professor of education at UCLA, has been quoted as saying, "She's left schools in Detroit in shambles. The lack of oversight, any accountability, is a huge problem and that seems to be the direction she wants to take education on a national level" (Abdul-Alim).

This should be music to the ears of those for-profit universities, which have weathered the Obama years. No question, private entities that currently provide or would like to provide education at any level, from preschool through the doctoral level, are crossing their fingers and licking their lips at the prospect of a Trump/DeVos team at the helm of the DOE. Whether that team delivers the relief, let alone the windfall, that the likes of Apollo Corporation no doubt hope for and anticipate, remains to be seen.

I should note that the Obama DOE remained relentless as 2016 came to a close. One provider that won't see a reversal of fortunes from Secretary DeVos is DeVry University. On December 15, 2016, the Federal Trade Commission announced that DeVry and its parent would pay $100 million to settle a suit brought by the FTC, alleging that the institution had misled prospective students (Federal Trade Commission). The agency's press release read as follows:

> Under the settlement resolving the FTC charges, DeVry will pay $49.4 million in cash to be distributed to qualifying students who were harmed by the deceptive ads, as well as $50.6 million in debt relief. The debt being forgiven includes the full balance owed—$30.35 million—on all private unpaid student loans that DeVry issued

to undergraduates between September 2008 and September 2015, and $20.25 million in student debts for items such as tuition, books and lab fees.

"When people are making important decisions about their education and their future, they should not be misled by deceptive employment and earnings claims," said FTC Chairwoman Edith Ramirez. "The FTC has secured compensation for the many students who were harmed, and I am pleased that DeVry is changing its practices."

The FTC's complaint charged that DeVry misled consumers in violation of the FTC Act by claiming that 90 percent of graduates actively seeking employment landed jobs in their field within six months of graduation. Advertisements making these claims appeared on television and radio, as well as online and in print and other media.

The complaint further alleges that DeVry misled students by claiming that graduates with bachelor's degrees, on average, had 15 percent higher incomes one year after graduation than the graduates with bachelor's degrees from all other colleges or universities.

The *proposed federal court order* requires DeVry to notify the students who will receive debt relief, and to inform the credit bureaus and collection agencies of the debt forgiveness. All loan and debt forgiveness will occur automatically. DeVry will also release transcripts and diplomas previously withheld from students because of outstanding debt and will cooperate with future requests for diplomas and transcripts and related enrollment or graduation information.

The settlement also includes provisions designed to prevent DeVry from misleading consumers in the future. Among other things, it prohibits DeVry from misrepresenting the likelihood that graduates will get a job as a result of their degree. It specifically prohibits DeVry from including jobs students obtained more than six months before graduating whenever DeVry advertises its graduates' success in finding jobs near graduation. The settlement also prohibits DeVry from misrepresenting the compensation or compensation ranges that students or graduates have received or can be expected to receive. (Federal Trade Commission)

For DeVry that money is gone. For the Apollo Education Group, the ACICS, and the for-profit sector of the higher education industry at large, pending actions taken in the Obama Administration's 11th hour remain ripe for reversal by the new American President and Secretary of Education. Indeed, the hated "Gainful Employment" regulations may well be open to revision or even rescission, as on June 30, 2017, DOE gave institutions extra time to comply. (US DOE VII)

The worm seems to have taken another turn. However, as I explain in Chapter Eight, Trump and DeVos are encountering the head winds of the so-called "deep state," i.e., the entrenched federal bureaucracy (including many employees protected by civil service laws and labor unions) that is to a significant degree impervious to regime changes.

Notes

1. In May 2017 Kaplan was sold to Purdue University.
2. Through much of 2016 a petition by a group of investors, seeking permission to take Apollo private, lay dormant at the DOE.
3. Notably, Trump's first choice for Secretary of Labor.

References

Abdul-Alim, Jamaal, "Experts Wary of Betsy DeVos as Education Secretary," *Diverse Issues in Higher Education*, December 1, 2016, accessed at http://diverseeducation.com/article/89868, December 28, 2016.
Apollo Education Group, Press Release, December 29, 2016, accessed at http://phx.corporate-ir.net/phoenix.zhtml?c=79624&p=irol-newsArticle&ID=2136316.
Burd, Stephen, "Bush's Proposals for a Second Term Would Favor Community Colleges and the For-Profit Sector," *Chronicle of Higher Education*, September 7, 2004, accessed at http://www.chronicle.com/article/Bushs-Proposals-for-a-Second/102004, December 29, 2016.
Castagnera, Jim, "Unable to Shake Qui Tam Case, University of Phoenix Faces Reappearance of Old Action," December 28, 2016, accessed at http://terrortrials.blogspot.com/2011/06/debate-about-student-debt-and-for.html
Cohen, Patricia, "For-Profit Colleges Accused of Fraud Still Receive U.S. Funds," *The New York Times*, October 12, 2015, accessed at http://www.nytimes.com/2015/10/13/business/for-profit-colleges-accused-of-fraud-still-receive-us-funds.html?_r=0, December 28, 2016.
Connolly, Amy R., "University of Phoenix Banned from Military Recruiting, DOD Investigating," UPI, October 10, 2015, accessed at http://www.upi.com/Top_News/US/2015/10/10/University-of-Phoenix-banned-from-military-recruiting-DOD-investigating/8161444482942, December 28, 2016.
"Corinthian Announces Cessation of Effectively All Operations," Corinthian Colleges, Inc., April 26, 2015, accessed at http://www.cci.edu/update.php, December 28, 2016.
Douglas-Gabriel, Danielle, "Education Secretary Ousts One of the Nation's Largest College Accreditors from Its Oversight Role," *Washington Post*, December 12, 2016, accessed at https://www.washingtonpost.com/news/grade-point/wp/2016/12/12/education-secretary-ousts-one-of-the-nations-largest-college-accreditors-from-its-oversight-role/?utm_term=.3355b2fc357f, December 28, 2016.
(Duncan I) Association of Private Colleges and Universities v. Duncan, 870 F.Supp. 2d 133 (D.D.C. 2012).
(Duncan II) Association of Private Sector Colleges & Universities v. Duncan, 110 F.Supp.3d 176 (D.D.C. 2015), affirmed 640 Fed. Appx. 5 (D.C. Cir. 2016).
Fain, Paul, "Vanishing Profit, and Campuses," *Inside Higher Ed*, May 7, 2015, accessed at https://www.insidehighered.com/news/2015/05/07/profit-chains-announce-new-wave-closures-and-sell-offs, December 28, 2016.

Federal Trade Commission, "Settlement Secures Financial Redress for Tens of Thousands of Students Harmed by Deceptive Ads that Touted Employment and Earning Potential," December 15, 2016, accessed at https://www.ftc.gov/news-events/press-releases/2016/12/devry-university-agrees-100-million-settlement-ftc, December 28, 2016.

Gonzales, Angela, "Apollo Group Settles Class Action Suit for $145 Million," *Phoenix Business Journal*, April 24, 2012, accessed at http://www.bizjournals.com/phoenix/news/2012/04/24/apollo-group-settles-class-action-suit.html, December 29, 2016.

Government Accountability Office, "FOR PROFIT COLLEGES: Undercover Testing Finds Colleges Encouraged Fraud and Engaged in Deceptive and Questionable Marketing Practices," GAO *Highlights*, GAO-10-948T, August 4, 2010, accessed at http://www.gao.gov/products/GAO-10-948T, December 29, 2016.

Hendow, United States ex rel. v. University of Phoenix, 461 F3d 1166 (9th Cir. 2006).

Korn, Melissa, "Department of Education Requires Letter of Credit for Apollo Education Privatization Deal," *Wall Street Journal*, December 7, 2016, accessed at http://www.wsj.com/articles/department-of-education-requires-letter-of-credit-for-apollo-education-privatization-deal-1481154088, December 28, 2016.

LaCroix, Kevin, "Two 2010 Securities Suits Filing Trends Converge," *The D&O Diary*, December 6, 2010, accessed at http://www.dandodiary.com/2010/12/articles/securities-litigation/two-2010-securities-suits-filing-trends-converge/, December 29, 2016.

Mufson, Steven and Jia Lynn Yang, "The Trials of Kaplan Higher Ed and the Education of The Washington Post Co.," *Washington Post*, April 9, 2011, accessed at https://www.washingtonpost.com/business/the-trials-of-kaplan-higher-ed-and-the-education-of-the-washington-post-co/2011/03/20/AFsGuUAD_story.html?utm_term=.5184db872688, December 29, 2016.

Rubenstein, Abigail, "U. of Phoenix Settles Qui Tam Suit for $78.5 M," *Law360*, December 14, 2009, accessed at http://www.law360.com/articles/139280/u-of-phoenix-settles-qui-tam-suit-for-78-5m, December 29, 2016.

Samuels, Alexander, "Feds Investigating Univ. of Phoenix for Possible Unfair Business Practices," *USA Today*, July 30, 2015, accessed at http://college.usatoday.com/2015/07/30/university-of-phoenix-federal-investigation/, December 28, 2016.

Sebastian, Michael, "The Donald Trump Appointment Tracker," *Marie Claire*, December 9, 2016, accessed at http://www.marieclaire.com/politics/a23922/donald-trump-cabinet-appointments/, December 28, 2016.

Smith, Ashley A., "Phoenix Owner Seeks Fresh Start," *Inside Higher Ed*, February 9, 2016, accessed at https://www.insidehighered.com/news/2016/02/09/apollos-new-owners-seek-fresh-start-beleaguered-company, December 28, 2016.

(US DOE I) "Proposed Rule Links Federal Student Aid to Loan Repayment Rates and Debt-to-Earnings Levels for Career College Graduates," U.S. Department of Education Press Office, July 23, 2010, accessed at https://www.ed.gov/news/press-releases/proposed-rule-links-federal-student-aid-loan-repayment-rates-and-debt-earnings-l, December 29, 2016.

(US DOE II) "U.S. Department of Education Heightens Oversight of Corinthian Colleges," U.S. Department of Education Press Office, June 19, 2014, accessed at http://www.ed.gov/

news/press-releases/us-department-education-heightens-oversight-corinthian-colleges, December 28, 2016.
(US DOE III) "U.S. Department of Education Signs Plan to Protect Students by Avoiding Immediate Closure of Corinthian Colleges," U.S. Department of Education Press Office, June 23, 2014, accessed at http://www.ed.gov/news/press-releases/us-department-education-signs-plan-protect-students-avoiding-immediate-closure-corinthian-colleges, December 28, 2016.
(US DOE IV) "U.S. Department of Education Accepts Operating Plan from Corinthian Colleges, Inc.," U.S. Department of Education Press Office, July 3, 2014, accessed at http://www.ed.gov/news/press-releases/us-department-education-accepts-operating-plan-corinthian-colleges-inc, December 28, 2016.
(US DOE V) "Education Department Names Seasoned Team to Monitor Corinthian Colleges," U.S. Department of Education Press Office, July 18, 2014, accessed at https://www.ed.gov/news/press-releases/education-department-names-seasoned-team-monitor-corinthian-colleges, December 19, 2016.
(US DOE VI) "U.S. Department of Education Fines Corinthian Colleges $30-Million for Misrepresentation," U.S. Department of Education Press Office, April 14, 2015, accessed at http://www.ed.gov/news/press-releases/us-department-education-fines-corinthian-colleges-30-million-misrepresentation, December 28, 2016.
(US DOE VII) "DeVos Presses Pause on Burdensome Gainful Employment Regulation," U.S. Department of Education Press Office, June 30, 2017, accessed at https://www.ed.gov/news/press-releases/devos-presses-pause-burdensome-gainful-employment-regulations, October 31, 2017.

· 5 ·

THE DECLINE OF NOT-FOR-PROFIT HIGHER EDUCATION

Clearly, the title of this chapter demands an immediate clarification in the nature of a narrowing. Not all nonprofit colleges and universities are in trouble. The Ivy League, most Research-One universities, and many elite, well-endowed liberal arts colleges are just fine, thank you.

But many more private colleges and universities are in trouble. In the Fall of 2016, more than 40 percent of nonprofit colleges and universities fell short of their enrollment goals, this despite an average 48 percent tuition discount rate (Hoover and Lipka). For many of the 2,300 private, nonprofit colleges and universities, which are in this circumstance, such a state of affairs might seem unsustainable. However, it's mighty hard to put a college out of business, as the following case studies—one old and one new—amply illustrate:

Case Study One: Hiwassee College

Hiwassee College links its early history very closely to the founding in 1826 of Tullagalla Academy, a school for boys, located in the Fork Creek Community some five miles from the site of college's present Tennessee campus. At about that time, a group of Methodist settlers set aside land near a fresh spring for a camp meeting that eventually came to be called the Bat Creek Campground.

Gradually, according to the college's website, a church and other structures were erected and used by believers who assembled annually for "camp meeting services." By 1845, the enrollment in the academy exceeded its capacity to accommodate the students. Consequently, the school moved to Bat Creek Campground and utilized the facilities available there.

When the academy director left in 1848, a group of five local Methodist leaders took over the school at the campgrounds, but raised its curriculum to the college level. Thus, in 1849, the current college was organized, replacing and expanding the academy's program. The new institution was named Hiwassee from the Cherokee word "ayuwasi," which (apparently quite economically) means "meadow place at the foot of the hills." The campus is in a beautiful region at the foothills of the Great Smoky Mountains. The founders selected as their first president, Dr. Robert E. Doak, a 25-year old Presbyterian "scholar." This choice was intended to signify that the emphasis at the College was to be on Christian education and "not on denominationalism."

Hiwassee College was chartered by the State of Tennessee in 1850 and initially admitted men, and later women, drawn primarily from the surrounding region. For many years, the school offered training all the way from elementary school right through the Bachelor's degree. At some periods in its history, the college also granted the Master's degree. Currently, Hiwassee College offers both Associate's and Bachelor's degrees.

Although always closely tied to the Methodist Church since its founding, it was not until 1908 that the Trustees of Hiwassee College and the Holston Conference of the Methodist Episcopal Church-South entered into an agreement for joint operation of the institution. At that time, the college was leased to the Holston Conference. A new charter was issued, and the school was reorganized as a junior college. Hiwassee College came under the complete control and ownership of the Methodist Church-South in 1937. Prior to 1980, the three United Methodist-related colleges in the Holston Conference (a geographic region that includes east Tennessee and small parts of southwest Virginia, and north Georgia) were governed by a unified Board of Trustees.

In 1980, the Board of Trustees established a separate Board of Governors for each college, and by 1990, each of the three schools operated under a separate, independent Board of Trustees. Today, Hiwassee is a coeducational, residential, liberal arts college, still affiliated with the Holston Conference of the United Methodist Church. Its campus has grown from the original seven acres donated by Reverend Daniel B. Carter to property comprised of eighteen buildings situated on sixty acres of a four-hundred acre tract of land located just one mile north of the town of Madisonville. It awards the Bachelor of Arts, Bachelor of Science, Associate of Arts, and Associate of Science degrees, and the Associate of Applied Science degree in a limited number of career/vocational fields (Hiwassee).

My first contact with Hiwassee College came in the guise of Dr. James Noseworthy in 2002 or '03, whom I met at a conference on disability law, organized by the University of New Hampshire's extension division in the District of Columbia. Serendipity put the two of us at the same conference table. We took a shine to one another and kept in touch. In August 2003, he wrote to tell me, "I have left the United Methodist Board of Higher Education and Ministry and now serve as president of …Hiwassee College…. I moved in February to a situation which is both challenging and delightful. I am glad to be back on campus working with such marvelous individuals as we shape the future of this college."

At the time, if the Southern Association of Colleges and Schools (SACS) had its way, Hiwassee had no future. The SACS Commission on Colleges was (and is) the accrediting body responsible for 11 southern states, including Tennessee. The SACS was seeking to yank Hiwasseee's accreditation on grounds of financial weakness. I interviewed Senior Fellow Jon Fuller of the National Association of Independent Colleges and Universities for a magazine piece on Hiwassee and other similarly beleaguered small, sectarian schools. Fuller commented that SACS was "the most rigid and bureaucratic of the six national accrediting organizations."

This was perhaps understandable, since Fuller continued, "The South has more fragile institutions as a percentage of its higher education stock than any other region of the country."

I soon learned that SACS had first accredited Hiwassee in 1958 and had most recently renewed in 2000. The Reaffirmation Committee had noted at the millennium that the college faced many "financial challenges." Issues cited in the report included deferred maintenance, projected revenue shortfalls, and interfund borrowing.

The SACS required a follow-up report. When that document failed to meet the accreditor's criteria, Hiwassee was issued a warning and required to submit yet another 12-month status report. After reviewing that second report in December 2002, SACS placed Hiwassee on probation. The beleaguered college submitted its third report in December 2003. Meanwhile, a "Special Committee" conducted a site visit to the campus.

The college's accreditation crisis came to a head on January 16, 2004, with the delivery of a SACS letter, which informed the Reverend Noseworthy and his staff, "With its upcoming review in December 2004, your institution will have exhausted its probationary status and its period of continued accreditation for good cause. At that time, the institution must be determined to be in compliance with all of the *Principles of Accreditation* or be removed from membership."

Yet another "Special Committee" visited Hiwassee in October 2004. The resulting report was damning. On December 4th, Hiwassee staff appeared at a Compliance Committee meeting, and the committee voted to remove accreditation. On February 24, 2005, an Appeals Committee affirmed academic capital punishment for Hiwassee (Castagnera).

However, reports of Hiwassee's demise proved premature. The college took its case into federal court. On March 22, 2005, Judge Thomas Vartan of the U.S. District Court for Eastern Tennessee issued a temporary restraining order, restoring Hiwassee's accreditation. "This is good news," Reverend Noseworthy understated at the time. The case then was transferred to the federal court for Northern Georgia, home to SACS headquarters.

On February 5, 2007, following extensive pretrial discovery and a hearing, Senior District Judge Owen Forrester issued his ruling. In many aspects, the 18-page decision went against Hiwassee. But His Honor also held that SACS must be held to common-law principles of fair play. He went on to find that a conflict of interest had occurred when, as a result of a family emergency, one Appeals Committee member was replaced by another, who was already a voting member of the Commission on Colleges. Having already voted once to yank Hiwassee's accreditation, that individual wasn't entitled to a second bite at the college's apple (Hiwassee I).

Noseworthy commented, "We have prevailed on one of the several issues in our case." True…but Judge Forrester found for SACS on many another issue. More ominous for the college was the district judge's observation that "it is significant to the court that Hiwassee has never front-on challenged the ultimate decision of SACS that Hiwassee failed to come into compliance…."

And, indeed, four months later, Judge Forrester ruled in SACS's favor on all the major issues in the case and lifted the temporary restraining order that had been in place since March 2005 (Hiwassee II). On appeal, His Honor's decision was affirmed (Hiwassee III).

So why is Hiwassee College alive and more or less well today? Simple: the college did what the for-profit universities, who lost their accreditor in 2016 to the heavy hammer of the Department of Education (see Chapter Four), have done; it found itself a new accreditor. On November 3, 2009, it attained candidacy status for accreditation as a Category II school with the Transnational Association of Christian Colleges and Schools. Full accreditation subsequently was attained through 2013, and this accreditation remains in place today (Wikipedia). It is also now accredited by the Council for Higher Education Accreditation (Hiwassee College II).

Case Study Two: Sweet Briar College

Hiwassee College is a case on point about how hard it is to kill a college that doesn't wish to die. Sweet Briar College is a case on point of a college that wasn't permitted to die, even after it attempted suicide.

Sweet Briar College is one of the last of a dying species: the all-women college. It recounts its history as follows:

> In a time when she wasn't even allowed to vote, Indiana Fletcher Williams wanted more for women. When she died in 1900, she left her estate to found an institution in memory of her only daughter, Daisy, who had died in 1884 at the age of 16. Indiana's wish was to prepare young women to "be useful members of society."
>
> Sweet Briar opened in 1906 with 51 students eager to build something new. The A.B. degree was immediately recognized by graduate programs at leading universities—and three of the College's first five graduates went on to pursue advanced degrees.

The site goes on to address the college's close call with permanent closure:

> In 2015, when an attempt was made to close Sweet Briar, our alumnae rose up and said, "no way." They fought a legal battle and raised more than $12 million in less than six months to preserve Sweet Briar's 114-year-old tradition of educating women who get things done. Like their 1906 predecessors, the students of Sweet Briar embraced the challenge of writing the College's next chapter.
>
> We're proud to say that today, the College is vibrant with new ideas, setting new trends, and shaping forward-thinkers. But we remember our beginnings and continue the traditions of the Honor Code and self-governance pioneered by Sweet Briar's very first class. Indiana's vision lives on in perpetuity—reaffirmed by today's students and alumnae who know firsthand just how precious it is. (Sweet Briar)

More than a century after its idealistic founding, on March 3, 2015, the school's board of trustees issued a stunning announcement: the college would close at the end of the summer session. The announcement cited "insurmountable financial challenges." With 700 students and an $84 million endowment, the college couldn't compete anymore, the board claimed (Anderson and Svrluga).

The cynical might ask whether the announcement reflected serious intentions or if the hidden agenda was to mobilize Sweet Briar's friends for a rescue. If the latter, it worked. Alumnae and friends formed a non-profit corporation, which they named Saving Sweet Briar. That organization, plus other students, parents, faculty, and staff united to sue the trustees. Even the local Commonwealth Attorney joined the action, which soon reached the Virginia Supreme Court. The court below had enjoined some of the actions necessary to operationalize the closure announcement, but refused to enjoin all such preparations. The Commonwealth Attorney appealed to the high court, which remanded the case back to the circuit judge on a legal technicality (Commonwealth).

As the lawsuits lingered in limbo, Virginia's Attorney General entered the melee and brokered a mediation agreement among the interested parties. After five weeks of talks, an agreement emerged, which included the following terms:

- Save Sweet Briar would raise and deliver $12 million within 60 days.
- The Attorney General would release restrictions on $16 million of college endowment, making the money available for ongoing operations.
- The embattled president agreed to resign, along with 13 of the 23 trustees (Kapsidelis; Virginia Government).

How did things work out? In January 2016, the admissions office announced it had received more than 1,000 applications for the fall term. The new leadership added that it hadn't needed to touch the 16 million (now unrestricted) endowment dollars freed up by the Virginia AG. To ease the cost of instruction, the college joined the Consortium for Online Humanities Instruction, thanks to a Council of Independent Colleges grant (Wikipedia).

Not All Are So Lucky

As the cliché goes, it remains to be seen whether Hiwassee and Sweet Briar will survive deep into the 21st century or if, conversely, they have only received brief reprieves. What is certain is that not all such small private colleges have been so lucky as have those two. As this book went to press, several small schools were identified in the media as on the chopping block, including

Burlington College in Vermont; Dowling College in Long Island (NY); and St. Catherine College in Kentucky (Biemiller).

Additionally, many more-substantial nonprofit universities are under extreme stress. For example, Rider University in central New Jersey (where I have spent some 21 years as the associate provost and legal counsel) found itself dangerously strapped for cash in 2016, as did many other tuition-driven, nonprofit, mid-sized universities across the country.

Forty percent of private colleges missed their enrollment goals for Fall 2016.

This is according to the Chronicle of Higher Education from its 4th annual survey of some 1,000 institutions. In a nutshell:

> As the number of high-school graduates dwindles, and their demographics shift, many colleges are struggling to attract enough students and cover expenses. More than four in 10 private colleges…missed their goals for enrollment and tuition revenue this year, according to the fourth annual *Chronicle* survey of small colleges and midsize public universities. In cooperation with the Council of Independent Colleges and the American Association of State Colleges and Universities, *The Chronicle* polled 1,063 colleges, of which 447 responded: 315 private and 132 public campuses. (Hoover and Lipka)

Can this be called a crisis? To some extent, this is a relative concept. According to Moody's, the average for the past decade has been five closures per year. Six closed in 2014. Beginning in 2018, predicts Moody's, the average will climb to 15 per year. Private schools with revenues below $100 million per year, and publics with gross annual income below $200 million are said to be the most vulnerable.

With tuition being the lifeblood of most of these small schools, an average discount rate of 48 percent—according to NACUBA—is probably an unsustainable business model for many of them. This average reduction from the sticker price has been steadily rising, and the data suggest that the bottom hasn't yet been plumbed.

Of course, the base is 2,300 nonprofit colleges and universities. So, one can easily argue that the loss of even 15 schools per year is hardly a crisis for this sector of the higher education industry as a whole. One might go so far as to characterize it as a natural response to shifting demographics and the weeding out of the weak members of the herd. Of course, it all depends on your perspective; if your college is among the casualties, you indeed may view this state of affairs as a crisis, or even a calamity.

It also depends upon whether the failure rate is on a shallow or a steep curve. If Moody's is right, then most nonprofit private universities can probably take a cautious rather than a crisis posture going forward. One way we might test Moody's forecast is to inquire into the causes of the current college failures.

One frequently cited reason that many small colleges are in trouble is their rural locales. President Richard Ekman of the Council of Independent Colleges has been quoted to the effect that, "As recently as a generation ago, the utopian small college in a small college town was the way to go for a lot of kids." But, he added, "Kids now seem to prefer metropolitan colleges. That's a factor every college in a remote location has to deal with" (Biemiller II). Okay, fine…if your school isn't rural, are you in the clear?

I mentioned my long-time employer, Rider University. With one campus located eight miles from New Jersey's capital, Trenton, and within an hour of New York and Philadelphia, rural location wasn't the issue. And with 4,000 students, "tiny" wasn't the issue either. While I can't violate my confidentiality obligations to my employer and client, I can repeat what was reported in the news media. This from NJ.com, October 29, 2015:

> LAWRENCE—Facing a potentially crippling budget crisis, Rider University will slash 13 majors and one minor and eliminate more than 20 jobs, including 14-full-time faculty members, the school announced today.
>
> The unprecedented budget cuts at the private liberal arts college are expected to save more than $2 million a year as Rider tries to close its deficit, already at $7.6 million of this year's $216 million budget, according to the university.
>
> Current juniors and seniors will be able to complete degrees in their major, but sophomores and freshman will need to switch majors or transfer. In total, 272 students, including 123 sophomores and freshman are in the affected programs, university President Gregory Dell'Omo said.
>
> "This is a tough day," Dell'Omo told NJ Advance Media after the town hall meeting. "But we would not have made this decision unless I really felt these were the right things for the university."
>
> The cuts were prompted by years of declining enrollment combined with rising costs for instruction, Dell'Omo said. But an official for the school's faculty union said the faculty and the university have a difference of opinion over the severity of Rider's financial challenges. (Clark)

Let it be said that the faculty union made some concessions and the layoffs were cancelled. But, what were the underlying causes of this crisis? Declining enrollments had resulted from increased competition, especially by aggressive public universities (see the profile presented in Chapter Three). Price outran what Dell'Omo liked to call "the value proposition." High costs of instruction, due principally to a series of unusually generous labor contracts with the faculty union, siphoned scarce dollars away from facilities and other amenities at a time when a billion-dollar bond issue enabled public-sector competitors like Montclair, Rowan and Rutgers universities to greatly enhance their physical plants. While these schools were building state-of-the-art "college town" projects, Rider was still trying to persuade students to pay for dorm rooms with no air conditioning.

In order to attract students under these circumstances, schools like Rider across the country discounted their tuitions by 40–50 percent, and sometimes even more. Such a business model is ultimately unsustainable, unless compensated by significantly reduced costs, enhanced auxiliary enterprise, and fund-raising income, and/or substantial enrollment increases. Otherwise, the inevitable result is drastic cuts one kind or another, to wit:

> PRINCETON—The president of Rider University has floated the idea of closing down the Westminster Choir College's campus and moving students to the university's main campus in Lawrence, the Rider News reported Tuesday.
>
> President Gregory Dell'Omo addressed the idea at two presentations last week, citing ongoing financial concerns at the university as a driving force behind the idea, the report said. The plan involves selling the choir college's current location in Princeton.
>
> Dell'Omo said Rider is also looking to increase enrollment, all in an effort to close a $13.1 million deficit by 2019. (Merriman)

The Rider University story strongly suggests that "tiny" and "rural" are not the whole story, and private-college closures may run at a larger rate than what Moody's imagines. However, I am pleased to report that, as this volume went to press, Rider had a three-pronged plan—sale of the Princeton campus and the choir college; concession bargaining with the faculty union; successful recruitment of a larger freshman class through precision pricing of tuition, room, and board—that promises financial recovery. I return to Rider in Chapter Nine.

And Then There Are the Regulations

My first stint as a higher-education administrator fell between 1974 and 1978. Based in the Department of University Communication at Cleveland's Case Western Reserve University, I served that R1 institution as an editor/writer and, after two promotions, as the director. I remember those 4.5 years as a time of significantly less government oversight than we live with today. Two examples should suffice.

Round about 1976 or 1977, I received a call from my boss, the executive vice president. Peter informed me that an anthropologist on the Western Reserve College faculty had a good story for me. I had my secretary set up an appointment and dutifully tramped from old main, across Euclid Avenue, to the Anthropology Department in a venerable stone building. Climbing the stairs, I detected a smell not unlike the one you may have encountered when opening your tackle box on the first day of trout season. Reaching the landing, I turned to the open door of Mohammed's office.

Staring at me from empty eye sockets from atop a four-drawer file cabinet was a mummy. Entering the office, I introduced myself to the mustachioed, dark-skinned professor seated at the desk. Invited to sit, I produced my notebook and heard his story. A specialist in nutritional issues, Mohammed had been conducting summer research among Native Americans somewhere in the Southwestern United States, when he came across the mummy in a burial cave, surrounded by the artifacts with which the Indian had been buried some hundreds or thousands of years ago. Popping the naturally mummified gent into the back of his pick-up truck, Mohammed had brought the old boy back with him to Cleveland.

Excited by the story, I contacted the late, great afternoon daily newspaper, the *Cleveland Press*. A photographer was dispatched to the Case campus. The next day, Mohammed's mummy was on the paper's front page. My buttons were popping.

Later that day, I got another phone call from the university's executive veep. Did I think there might be some blowback from the Native American community? After all, Chief Wahoo, the Cleveland Indian's mascot, was already a target of Native American wrath all those 40 years ago. Gee, Peter, I was so excited about a front page in a major daily that the thought had never crossed my mind.

Think you know the outcome of this story? Think again: we never heard a discouraging word from any American Indian or any Native American organization. Nor did any federal agency raise a cry of protest. What could, and undoubtedly today, would be branded as grave robbery raised no eyebrows four decades back. Back then, higher ed operated in a very different regulatory environment, indeed.

Need more convincing? Same four-year stint, separate setting: A group of materials scientists in CWRU's Case Institute of Technology received a

$4.2 million NSF grant to develop artificial arteries. A Cleveland TV station indicated interest in doing an evening-news piece. I brought them to the Principal Investigator's lab. Anxious for some visual interest, the TV reporter inquired about how the arteries would be tested.

"We test them in rats," came the PI's reply.

The reporter's eyes brightened. Rats were visual. And so the lights and camera were set up in front of a lab table. The PI produced a rat in what appeared to me to be a Tupperware container.

"How do you handle them?"

"Oh, we pick them up by their tails." And with that, my scientist hoisted his specimen from the container by its tail. What happened next can only be described as the rat going "ratshit." Spinning and gyrating madly under the alien spotlights, the rodent dropped to the table and scurried to the floor and off into the shadows.

Smiling into the camera, the PI held the pinkish appendage between thumb and forefinger and pronounced, "He unscrewed himself from his tail."

Needless to say, we made both the six o'clock and eleven o'clock news broadcasts. And—you get the idea—not a squeal nor a bark out of the animal-rights establishment.

Nor any protest from the NSF or any other federal or state agency. A different regulatory environment, indeed, indeed.

My, Oh My, How Times Have Changed

Fast forward 40 years. Federal regulatory activity directed at higher education and a concomitant bloating of the size and cost of college administration can be traced to two events in my opinion. The first was the September 11, 2001 terrorist attacks. The second was the election of a Democratic president in November 2008.

The U.S. Senate Task Force on Federal Regulation of Higher Education issued its report in February 2015. Less than two years earlier, when the bi-partisan study group was formed, a November 2013 press released explained it mission.

> WASHINGTON, Nov. 18—Senate education committee Ranking Member Senator Lamar Alexander (R-Tenn.), and members Barbara Mikulski (D-Md.), Richard Burr (R-N.C.), and Michael Bennet (D-Colo.) today announced the formation of a task force to examine burdens on institutions of higher education.

The Task Force on Government Regulation of Higher Education will conduct a comprehensive review of federal regulations and reporting requirements affecting colleges and universities and make recommendations to reduce and streamline regulations, while protecting students, institutions and taxpayers.

Alexander said: "Let's face it: the federal government has become one of the greatest obstacles to innovation in higher education. The stack of federal regulations on colleges and universities today is not the result of evildoers, it is simply the piling up of well-intentioned laws and regulations without anyone spending an equal amount of time weeding the garden first. This task force will help Congress weed the garden."

Mikulski said: "In order for America to out-build and out-innovate the rest of the world, we must first out-educate. And part of out-educating is making sure that we are supporting our institutions of higher education—helping them be them as they work to educate our next generation. Over the years, I have heard concerns from these institutions regarding federal requirements that, while well intentioned, often end up being duplicative and burdensome. I have committed to seeing what can be done. We need to regulate, not strangulate. As this Task Force works on a path forward, it will be well-served through the leadership of the University System of Maryland's own Dr. William 'Brit' Kirwan, bringing with him a wealth of knowledge and experience."

Burr said: "The tidal wave of regulations and reporting requirements faced by colleges and universities today is stifling innovation and, worse, raising college tuition price tags as schools pass on these compliance costs to students. This task force will assemble experts and stakeholders to help streamline regulations and reduce the unnecessary burdens on institutions of higher education."

Bennet said: "We must create an environment where our colleges and universities are focused on doing what they do best, and that's educating students to succeed in the 21st century economy. To do that, we must to take a step back and consider how the current requirements are helping or affecting that goal. This task force offers the opportunity to take a broad look at federal regulations and requirements in order to inform our reauthorization of the Higher Education Act. What we need is a system that makes sense for students and for colleges and universities."

The task force is co-chaired by Nicholas Zeppos, chancellor of Vanderbilt University, and William Kirwan, chancellor of the University System of Maryland. It will comprise 14 college and university presidents and higher education experts. The American Council on Education will provide organizational assistance.

In letters to request participation in the task force, the senators wrote: "Our higher education system remains the best in the world and is often credited for its breadth of choice and commitment to institutional autonomy. Over the past decade, however, Congress and the U.S. Department of Education have added more mandates, reporting requirements and regulations with which institutions must comply. This Task Force creates an opportunity to conduct a comprehensive review of federal regulations and reporting requirements affecting colleges and universities and make recommendations to Congress and the Administration to streamline and reduce federal regulations, while at the same time maintaining student and taxpayer protections." (U.S. Senate)

Mission accomplished? I doubt it. A 2015 Vanderbilt University study concluded that federal regulation costs higher education $27 billion a year (Stratford).

The "Sexual Assault" Crusade

The final section of this chapter is focused on a single, over-arching litigation issue, which I think it's safe to say has been in recent years the most controversial and costly intrusion of the federal government onto our campuses. It alone has bred litigation and disruption out of all proportions to regulatory requirements, in general. Of course, I am speaking about the campaign that commenced in a September 2014 speech by President Obama, calling for the eradication of sexual assault on college campuses. Christened his "It's On Us" speech, Mr. Obama's remarks were in pertinent part as follows:

> An estimated one in five women has been sexually assaulted during her college years—one in five. Of those assaults, only 12 percent are reported, and of those reported assaults, only a fraction of the offenders are punished....
>
> For anybody whose once-normal, everyday life was suddenly shattered by an act of sexual violence, the trauma, the terror can shadow you long after one horrible attack. It lingers when you don't know where to go or who to turn to. It's there when you're forced to sit in the same class or stay in the same dorm with the person who raped you; when people are more suspicious of what you were wearing or what you were drinking, as if it's your fault, not the fault of the person who assaulted you. It's a haunting presence when the very people entrusted with your welfare fail to protect you....
>
> It insults our most basic values as individuals and families, and as a nation. We are a nation that values liberty and equality and justice. And we're a people who believe every child deserves an education that allows them to fulfill their God-given potential, free from fear of intimidation or violence. And we owe it to our children to live up to those values. ...
>
> It is on all of us to reject the quiet tolerance of sexual assault and to refuse to accept what's unacceptable. (White House)

The Underlying Legal Foundation

The Department of Education, acting through its Office of Civil Rights, took the lead in operationalizing Mr. Obama's campaign. The OCR already had a legal theory in place. Witness the following 2011 "Dear Colleague" letter in which OCR already had asserted authority over campus sexual-assault case via a federal statute long believed to apply primarily to gender parity in college athletics.

Dear Colleague:

Education has long been recognized as the great equalizer in America. The U.S. Department of Education and its Office for Civil Rights (OCR) believe that providing all students with an educational environment free from discrimination is extremely important. The sexual harassment of students, including sexual violence, interferes with students' right to receive an education free from discrimination and, in the case of sexual violence, is a crime.

Title IX of the Education Amendments of 1972 (Title IX), 20 U.S.C. §§ 1681 et seq., and its implementing regulations, 34 C.F.R. Part 106, prohibit discrimination on the basis of sex in education programs or activities operated by recipients of Federal financial assistance. Sexual harassment of students, which includes acts of sexual violence, is a form of sex discrimination prohibited by Title IX. In order to assist recipients, which include school districts, colleges, and universities (hereinafter "schools" or "recipients") in meeting these obligations, this letter explains that the requirements of Title IX pertaining to sexual harassment also cover sexual violence, and lays out the specific Title IX requirements applicable to sexual violence. Sexual violence, as that term is used in this letter, refers to physical sexual acts perpetrated against a person's will or where a person is incapable of giving consent due to the victim's use of drugs or alcohol. An individual also may be unable to give consent due to an intellectual or other disability. A number of different acts fall into the category of sexual violence, including rape, sexual assault, sexual battery, and sexual coercion. All such acts of sexual violence are forms of sexual harassment covered under Title IX.

The statistics on sexual violence are both deeply troubling and a call to action for the nation. A report prepared for the National Institute of Justice found that about 1 in 5 women are victims of completed or attempted sexual assault while in college. The report also found that approximately 6.1 percent of males were victims of completed or attempted sexual assault during college. According to data collected under the Jeanne Clery Disclosure of Campus Security and Campus Crime Statistics Act (Clery Act), 20 U.S.C. § 1092(f), in 2009, college campuses reported nearly 3,300 forcible sex offenses as defined by the Clery Act. This problem is not limited to college. During the 2007–2008 school year, there were 800 reported incidents of rape and attempted rape and 3,800 reported incidents of other sexual batteries at public high schools. Additionally, the likelihood that a woman with intellectual disabilities will be sexually assaulted is estimated to be significantly higher than the general population. The Department is deeply concerned about this problem and is committed to ensuring that all students feel safe in their school, so that they have the opportunity to benefit fully from the school's programs and activities.

This letter begins with a discussion of Title IX's requirements related to student-on-student sexual harassment, including sexual violence, and explains schools' responsibility to take immediate and effective steps to end sexual harassment and sexual violence. These requirements are discussed in detail in OCR's *Revised Sexual Harassment Guidance* issued in 2001 (*2001 Guidance*). This letter supplements the *2001 Guidance* by providing additional guidance and practical examples regarding the Title IX requirements as they relate to sexual violence. This letter concludes by discussing the proactive efforts schools can take to prevent sexual harassment and violence, and by providing examples of remedies that schools and OCR may use to end such conduct, prevent its recurrence, and address its effects. Although some examples contained in this letter are applicable only in the postsecondary context, sexual harassment and violence also are concerns for school districts. The Title IX obligations discussed in this letter apply equally to school districts unless otherwise noted.

Title IX Requirements Related to Sexual Harassment and Sexual Violence
Schools' Obligations to Respond to Sexual Harassment and Sexual Violence
Sexual harassment is unwelcome conduct of a sexual nature. It includes unwelcome sexual advances, requests for sexual favors, and other verbal, nonverbal, or physical conduct of a sexual nature. Sexual violence is a form of sexual harassment prohibited by Title IX.

As explained in OCR's *2001 Guidance*, when a student sexually harasses another student, the harassing conduct creates a hostile environment if the conduct is sufficiently serious that it interferes with or limits a student's ability to participate in or benefit from the school's program. The more severe the conduct, the less need there is to show a repetitive series of incidents to prove a hostile environment, particularly if the harassment is physical. Indeed, a single or isolated incident of sexual harassment may create a hostile environment if the incident is sufficiently severe. For instance, a single instance of rape is sufficiently severe to create a hostile environment.

Title IX protects students from sexual harassment in a school's education programs and activities. This means that Title IX protects students in connection with all the academic, educational, extracurricular, athletic, and other programs of the school, whether those programs take place in a school's facilities, on a school bus, at a class or training program. (Office of Civil Rights)

As the OCR pressed the campaign forward, schools that lacked appropriate policies hastened to put them into place...or were driven to do so by complaints filed with and investigated by the OCR. Let me be clear: no higher-ed institution can afford to be without an adequate set of policies and procedures. For smaller schools in particular, this may mean the difference between stability on one hand and a financial/PR/legal crisis on the other.

It took little more than a year from President Obama's 2014 speech for the media to identify a trend in litigation against universities by students accused of sexual assault. In November 2015, *Inside Higher Ed* reported, "Last week, Brandon Austin, a former college basketball player, filed a lawsuit against the University of Oregon for $7.5 million, arguing that administrators were violating his rights when they suspended him over his alleged involvement in a gang rape" (New).

The article went on the quote Director Samantha Harris of the Foundation for Individual Rights in Education to the effect that, "Almost every week, there's at least one more suit like this. It's a very rapidly emerging area of the law" (New).

By early 2017, commentators in the *Washington Post* would report, "The system currently in place at colleges and universities runs far too great a risk of innocent students being found guilty. A recent study from UCLA's John Villasenor estimated that as many as 1 in 3 innocent students suffer this fate. The actual percentage is likely higher, since Villasenor's study couldn't take into account some aspects of the college process (such as the ability of the accuser to appeal not-guilty findings and the lack of direct cross-examination at most schools) that increase the chances of a finding of guilt" (Johnson and Taylor).

Johnson and Taylor illustrate their point with an example from their own book:

> We lead the book, for instance, with a case at Amherst, in which the accusing student sent multiple texts on the night of the incident talking about her need to construct a lie. (The male student was the boyfriend of the accuser's roommate, who was out of town for the weekend.) Amherst initially didn't discover the texts, because the college couldn't subpoena the accuser's phone and didn't bother to ask her regular correspondents if they had any texts from her. When the accused student tracked down the students to whom his accuser had texted, the college said he had produced the evidence too late. He then sued, and in a deposition the college's hired investigator said she was interested only in evidence that *corroborated* the accuser's account—not in evidence showing that the accuser had lied. (Johnson and Taylor)

Let it be said that Obama and his Department of Education launched their crusade with the best of intentions. We know that alcohol abuse, hazing, and sexual assault are ongoing issues on college campuses down the decades to the present day. We know that it is difficult and often traumatic for the victims of sexual assault to get justice in our law courts. Witness, for instance, the long Odyssey of Bill Cosby's many victims. Nonetheless, we must ask if making the victim's path to "justice" wider and straighter worth the abrogation of fundamental civil liberties. To what, specifically, am I referring?

TABLE 5.1: Comparison of the Criminal Justice and the Collegiate Justice Systems.

Criminal Justice System	Collegiate Justice System
Proof of Guilt: Beyond a Reasonable Doubt	Proof of Guilt: More Likely Than Not
Cross-examination of the accuser and adverse witnesses	Typically no cross-examination. Accused's attorney may be present but must submit questions to the adjudication panel, who can decide whether or not to ask them

Criminal Justice System	Collegiate Justice System
Lack of accuser's consent must be proved by the police and prosecutor	Affirmative consent by the accuser must be proved by the accused
Fourth and 14th Amendment search and seizure rules apply to police investigations, notably a finding of probable cause by a warrant-issuing judge	At private colleges and universities, public safety officers can conduct searches with the approval of a student affairs representative
The Fifth and 14th Amendments protect the accused from compelled testimony against himself	Refusal to respond to an accusation or fully cooperate with the investigation and adjudication will be interpreted as indicia of guilt

Source: Author.

These deficiencies don't pertain to every institution of higher education, but they are typical, so far as I am aware. One upshot is "the dozens of lawsuits filed by accused students in the past few years" (Johnson and Taylor). Not only are the lawsuits proliferating. Additionally, they often include university officials, such as the dean of students, as named defendants. And the cost? Putting aside the dollar and HR costs of serving as police, judge, and jury in these cases, settlements alone are significant. In mid-2016, *USA Today* reported, "The $2.48 million payout to end a sexual assault lawsuit against the University of Tennessee is the latest in a spate of settlements entered into by colleges and universities across the country faced with a growing number of similar legal challenges in recent years.... One expert in Title IX...says the $2.48 million settlement in the UT case is a 'good deal' for the university, which estimated it could spend up to $5.5 million in legal fees defending the case, which was scheduled for trial in 2018" (Wadhwani).

I could go on and on in an already-lengthy chapter, chronicling the specifics of due process abuse and litigation costs. Instead, let me refer you to Johnson and Taylors's book (Johnson and Taylor II).

We saw in Chapter Four that several once-mighty for-profit firms were obliterated by regulatory enforcement actions during the Obama Administration. While the nonprofit sector doesn't face such an existential threat from the regulatory burden, that burden may well be the bale of straw that breaks the camel's back. Is relief in sight? I attempt an answer to that question in Chapter Eight.

References

Anderson, Nick and Susan Svrluga, "Sweet Briar College to Close Because of Financial Challenges," *Washington Post*, March 3, 2015, accessed at https://www.washingtonpost.com/news/grade-point/wp/2015/03/03/sweet-briar-college-to-close-because-of-financial-challenges/?utm_term=.545992d01227

Biemiller, Lawrence, "3 Small Colleges Close. Is That a Trend?" *Chronicle of Higher Education*, June 2, 2016, accessed at http://chronicle.com/article/3-Small-Colleges-Close-Is/236677?cid

Biemiller, Lawrence, "Small, Rural Colleges Grapple with Their Geography," *Chronicle of Higher Education*, June 10, 2016, accessed at http://chronicle.com/article/Sall-Rural-Colleges-Grapple/236761

Castagnera, Jim, "Mice That Roar: Small, Sectarian Colleges Resist Efforts to Extinguish Them," *Greentree Gazette*, May 2007, at 28.

Clark, Adam, "Rider University Slashing 13 Majors, Laying Off Professors," NJ.com, October 29, 2015, accessed at http://www.nj.com/education/2015/10/rider_university_slashing_13_majors_laying_off_pro.html

Commonwealth ex rel. Bowyer v. Sweet Briar Institute, 2015 WL 3646914 (Va. Supr.)

Hiwassee College, "Accreditation," accessed at https://hiwassee.edu/academics/accreditation

Hiwassee College, "History," accessed at https://www.hiwassee.edu/about-us/history

Hiwassee College, Inc. v. Southern Association of Colleges and Schools, Inc., 2007 WL 433098 (U.S.D.Ct., N.D.Ga.) (Hiwassee I).

Hiwassee College, Inc. v. Southern Association of Colleges and Schools, Inc., 490 F. Supp. 2d 1348 (N.D.Ga. 2007).

Hiwassee College, Inc. v. Southern Association of Colleges and Schools, Inc., 531 F. 3d 1333 (11th Cir. 2008).

"Hiwassee College," *Wikipedia*, accessed at https://en.wikipedia.org/wiki/Hiwassee_College

Hoover, Eric and Sara Lipka, "Enrollment Goals Remain Elusive for Small Colleges," *Chronicle of Higher Education*, December 11, 2016, accessed at http://www.chronicle.com/article/Enrollment-Goals-Remain/238624

Johnson, K.C. and Stuart Taylor, Jr., *The Campus Rape Frenzy: The Attack on Due Process at America's Universities* (New York: Encounter Books 2017).

Johnson, K.C. and Stuart Taylor, "The Dangers of Gutting Due Process in Campus Sexual Assault Cases," *Washington Post*, January 30, 2017, accessed at https://www.washingtonpost.com/news/volokh-conspiracy/wp/2017/01/30/the-dangers-of-gutting-due-process-in-campus-sexual-assault-cases/?utm_term=.3cda3fbd302a

Kapsidelis, Karin, "Agreement Reached to Keep Sweet Briar Open," *Richmond Times-Dispatch*, June 20, 2015, accessed at http://www.richmond.com/news/virginia/article_4b2f03d8-a089-5f8c-9c39-6faa19da07ce.html

Merriman, Anna, "Rider U. Suggests Closing Westminster Choir Campus in Princeton, Report Says," NJ.com, December 7, 2016, accessed at http://www.nj.com/mercer/index.ssf/2016/12/rider_u_considers_closing_princeton_campus.html

New, Jake, "Court Wins for Accused," *Inside Higher Ed*, November 5, 2015, accessed at *National Pan-Hellenic Council*, http://www.zphib1920.org/policy/NPHC%20Joint%20Position%20 Statement%20Against%20Hazing%20(2003).pdf

Office of Civil Rights, U.S. Department of Education, "Dear Colleague" Letter (2011), accessed at http://www2.ed.gov/about/offices/list/ocr/letters/colleague-201104.html

Ryan, Joe, "Defendant in Fatal Hazing at Rider Takes a Plea Deal," *Newark Star-Ledger*, October 17, 2008, accessed at http://www.nj.com/news/index.ssf/2008/10/defendant_in_fatal_hazing_at_r.html

Stratford, Michael, "Vandy Takes on Federal Regs, Redux," *Inside Higher Ed*, October 19, 2015, accessed at https://www.insidehighered.com/news/2015/10/19/vanderbilt-study-again-highlights-what-colleges-view-burdensome-federal-regulations

Sweet Briar College, "History," accessed at http://sbc.edu/about/history/

U.S. Senate Committee on Health, Education, Labor & Pensions, "Senate Education Committee Members Announce Task Force to Review Higher Ed Regulations and Reporting Requirements, " November 18, 2013, accessed at http://www.help.senate.gov/chair/newsroom/press/senate-education-committee-members-announce-task-force-to-review-higher-ed-regulations-and-reporting-requirements

Taylor, Stuart and K.C. Johnson, "DeVos will Restore Due Process on Campus Assault," *USA Today*, January 31, 2017, accessed at https://www.usatoday.com/story/opinion/2017/01/31/sexual-assault-on-campus-due-process-betsy-devos-column/97239118/

Virginia Government, Memorandum of Understanding (Sweet Briar College), June 20, 2015, accessed at http://ag.virginia.gov/files/06_20_15_-_MOU.pdf

White House, "President Obama Launches the 'It's On Us' Campaign to End Sexual Assault on Campus," September 10, 2014, accessed at https://obamawhitehouse.archives.gov/blog/2014/09/19/president-obama-launches-its-us-campaign-end-sexual-assault-campus

Wikipedia, "Sweet Briar College," accessed at https://en.wikipedia.org/wiki/Sweet_Briar_College#cite_note-16

Part Two
Some Possible Solutions

· 6 ·
ADDRESSING THE COST OF INSTRUCTION

Breaking the "Death Spiral" of Tuition Discounting via the "Value Proposition"

Three key facts of life drive this discussion.

First, most colleges and universities depend primarily upon tuition, and related room, board, and fees, for most of their revenues.

Second, most colleges and universities lack "an historic, strong or differentiated brand position…" (McGee, p. 67).

Third, "many…colleges and universities turn to the most powerful and efficient market tool they have to reach their goals: price manipulation. A college can induce demand for an undifferentiated product by effectively manipulating its price" (McGee, p. 68).

As with most things in life and business, the devil hides in the details. While tuition has repeatedly outrun inflation, gross tuition increases have been offset by tuition discounts (Selingo). Thus, "a poorly employed race-to-the-bottom pricing strategy comes with its own price—limited (or sometimes nonexistent) growth in revenue from tuition and difficulty in managing retention…" (McGee, p. 69). At least 90 percent of students at 69 percent of schools responding to a recent NACUBO survey were receiving tuition discounts (EAB). In academic year 2015–2016, the average freshman discount rate reached 48.6 percent (Seltzer).

Tuition discounting (aka financial aid or euphemistically "scholarships") can't be eliminated. It is, and must remain, a major weapon in our arsenal. But, carrying through with this metaphor, the weapon must be a rifle, not a shotgun. "Many companies that specialize in financial aid consulting have found that the highest yields among admitted students can come from those who are neither the highest academic achievers nor the most in financial need." (Matthews et al., p. 66)

> The so-called 'B' students from middle-income families often tend to get ignored when allocating limited grant aid. They are not academically distinguished enough for the scholarships aimed at great performance, and they are not financially needy enough for the grant aid set aside for low income. (Matthews et al., p. 66)

And yet "these middle-of-the-continuum students are often the most likely to choose the institution as their first preference" (Matthews et al., p. 66).

If these assertions are accurate, then many nondistinctive schools—the audience I am hoping most to reach with this book—will be well advised to aim their tuition-discount rifles at this student demographic: "B" students from middle-class families.

The way to hit the target is by enhancing what one college president I know calls "The Value Proposition." It's hard to be distinctive—to offer or appear to offer value for dollars that is greater than that offered (or apparently offered) by competitors with all the same academic programs and physical amenities. Or, as Gilbert and Sullivan say in "The Gondoliers," when everyone is somebody, then no one's anybody; when everyone offers much the same menu of majors and master's degrees, we are all in the same gondola.

We might take a look at some "A-Plus Schools for B Students" (U.S. News I). U.S. News selected the colleges and universities to be included on its list by the following methodology:

- All had to be ranked in the top three-fourths of their categories of 2017 Best Colleges.
- All had to have at least a 75 percent freshman-to-sophomore retention record.
- All had to have no more than half of their first-year students placed in the top 10 percent of their high school classes, and no more than 80

percent of their first-year students placed in the top 25 percent of their high school classes.
- All matriculated students had to have an SAT 75th percentile score of 1,350 or lower (U.S. News II).

For our purposes, let's refine this methodology by an additional criterion: student-body size. Thus, from the 310 schools on the U.S. News list, I've chosen four such schools that have student bodies below 10,000.

(1) Clark University: "Clark University is a private institution that was founded in 1887. It has a total undergraduate enrollment of 2,397, its setting is city, and the campus size is 50 acres. It utilizes a semester-based academic calendar. Clark University's ranking in the 2017 edition of Best Colleges is National Universities, 74. Its tuition and fees are $43,150 (2016–17)." (Clark) That's a hefty price tag. So where's the "Value Proposition"?

"Clark University in Worcester, Mass., is a small liberal arts institution in the midst of 11 other colleges and universities. Together, the schools make up the Higher Education Consortium of Central Massachusetts. All Clark students can get a WOO card: a pass that grants discounts at area attractions, baseball games, and the local ski slope, Wachusett Mountain. Clark students can also ride the free intercampus shuttle to Becker College, Worcester Polytechnic Institute, Assumption College, Worcester State University, and College of the Holy Cross" (Clark).

"HECCMA college students benefit from a plethora of course offerings at a number of our member institutions. Cross-registration enriches the college experience by providing students with an opportunity to take courses at other member institutions, both public and private, to access additional opportunities for knowledge" (HECCMA).

(2) Fordham University: "Fordham University is a private institution that was founded in 1841. It has a total undergraduate enrollment of 8,855, its setting is urban, and the campus size is 93 acres. It utilizes a semester-based academic calendar. Fordham University's ranking in the 2017 edition of Best Colleges is National Universities, 60. Its tuition and fees are $47,317 (2015–16)" (Fordham).

"At Fordham University, 'New York is [your] campus' as the school's website says. With campuses throughout New York City, students live and learn in the thick of an urban experience. The school's original Bronx campus, Rose Hill, is in walking distance to the Bronx Zoo, New York Botanical Gardens and Little Italy. Today, Fordham has two more campuses: Lincoln Center, which is close to Central Park, and Westchester campus, which is in West Harrison, N.Y." (Fordham).

(3) Howard University: "Howard University is a private institution that was founded in 1867. It has a total undergraduate enrollment of 6,883, its setting is urban, and the campus size is 258 acres. It utilizes a semester-based academic calendar. Howard University's ranking in the 2017 edition of Best Colleges is National Universities, 124. Its tuition and fees are $24,908 (2016–17)" (Howard).

"At Howard University, a historically black college in the heart of the District of Columbia, all undergraduate students complete a university wide core curriculum. Required courses include those in English composition and Afro-American studies. Students then have dozens of majors to choose from, including Afro-American studies, French, and music therapy. Outside of class, Howard students may choose to get involved in one of the school's many student organizations, including fraternities and sororities and academic clubs" (Howard).

(4) University of San Francisco: "University of San Francisco is a private institution that was founded in 1855. It has a total undergraduate enrollment of 6,782, its setting is urban, and the campus size is 55 acres. It utilizes a 4-1-4-based academic calendar. University of San Francisco's ranking in the 2017 edition of Best Colleges is National Universities, 107. Its tuition and fees are $44,494 (2016–17)" (USF).

"The University of San Francisco is a Jesuit institution in California's Bay Area. The school tries to emphasize its Jesuit mission in every degree program offered. Students participate in service-learning courses, during which academic coursework is complemented by volunteer work around San Francisco. The university at large is committed to bettering the community, including through partnerships with local organizations and work through the school's research centers and institutes. More than 90 percent of freshmen live in on-campus housing" (USF).

What do these four small–medium schools have in common? I contend that each has found a way of distinguishing itself from the pack and thus enhancing its "Value Proposition" for a targeted student population. Its gondola has set a course that helps it stand out from the fleet. Clark offers a smorgasbord of institutions, where classes can be taken and student life pursued outside the classroom. Clark has created a virtual megaversity beyond its own campus boundaries. Fordham has done something similar. It has made one of the greatest cities on the planet its campus.

Howard and USF focus on race and religion, respectively. Students of color who value that identity know that Howard is, and long has been, the best of the Historically Black Colleges. USF, bucking the 21st-century secularization trend, has returned to its Catholic roots. Not only Catholic students, but others who seek an education grounded in a religious ethos, are assured they can find it at USF.

Note what each of these schools has done. First, as *U.S. News* points out, it has chosen to target "B students." In a down-slope demographic environment, the best schools will get the best students. We who are below that top tier must seek our fair share from the fat midriff of the bell curve. And, then, how do we attract that fair share? By projecting a distinction that enhances our "Value Proposition."

This can be location, or connections, or religion, or culture, or combinations of several such attributes. These examples are not exhaustive.

Once the appropriate demographic has been identified, and the applications have been gathered, it remains to close the deal. In the words of a financial-aid colleague of mine, every admission/aid offer today turns into a negotiation. Parents have become savvy consumers. When I was a high school student in the mid-1960s, my parents—both of whom lacked even a high school education—knew they wanted their kids to get college degrees. They had little in the way of resources to contribute toward that aspiration, and even less idea where they wanted us to go. For my part, enjoying little by way of guidance from my high school counselor (who told me, "You should apply to a Catholic college. I drove by La Salle once and it looked nice."), I applied to a college attended by a favorite cousin (Franklin & Marshall) and, yes, La Salle.

In 2017–2018, the Common Application is just one reason high school students may apply to a dozen or more schools. Many, after being admitted, may even pony up the deposit required to hold a seat, while continuing to shop the competition for a better deal. The colleges for their part will try to shape financial-aid packages to build an incoming class of the size and shape most desired. Allentown (PA)'s Muhlenberg College explains it this way:

> Preferential packaging means, simply, that the students a college would most like to enroll will receive the most advantageous financial aid packages. Financial aid packages are made up of:
> - Grants. These may come from the college, the state, or the national government. They are "gifts," or "free money" and do not have to be paid back.
> - Loans. You are entitled to some government loans, and there are others you or your parents must qualify for, but taking loans is always optional. Loans must be repaid, usually beginning six months after graduation from college.
> - Work. Colleges and the government both fund on-campus work programs. These programs are designed to help a student meet the total cost of attending college—over and above tuition and fees—in exchange for on-campus work.
>
> A preferential financial aid package includes a far greater percentage of grant aid than self-help (loans and work). Because they have discretion over how much grant aid they choose to award a student, a college can award a bigger grant to a student it would really like to enroll. In some

cases, the total of grant from the college and the loans the student is entitled to may exceed the student's financial need. (Muhlenberg)

The problem with this explanation, aimed at students visiting the college's website, is that it implies a measure of institutional control, which is no longer enjoyed by most schools below the top tier or two. More and more of us are finding we need to make the grant (tuition-discount) piece of the package ever larger for an ever-larger percentage of the pool of acceptable (never mind desirable) applicants.

Additionally, many of these targeted students do not deem us to be their first choice. In other words, after closing the deal with those students most desirable to us—presumably the same students who are drawn to us by our particular articulation of the "Value Proposition"—we still need more students. Of course, we will try to sell them on that "Value Proposition." This may succeed in some cases, but that may still not be enough.

For a significant (and, I suggest, a growing) number of colleges and universities, filling the class to the budgeted projection means a lot of those individual negotiations to which my colleague in financial aid was referring. It's no exaggeration to say that the entering class is built student-by-student.

A stark example is Sweet Briar College, the case study I presented in Chapter Five. That case study ended with a court order directing the trustees to keep the college open. The sequel started with Phillip C. Stone, a retired college president and semiretired attorney, who in July 2015 was elected the college's new president by telephone and who arrived on campus with "a garment bag and a suitcase full of white shirts." Stone moved into a nearby motel, because his predecessor still occupied the presidential house (Kolowich).

> Sweet Briar's doors were open. The new administration would now have to walk students over the threshold, one by one. [Steven W. Nape, an enrollment consultant retained by Stone] handled a lot of the more technical questions about financial aid. Sometimes, families wanted to talk to the president himself, and he obliged. Mr. Nape quickly learned to pass skeptical parents to Marcia Thom-Kaley, a longtime music professor who just had been named a trustee, and had a knack for moving them with impassioned monologues about the resilience of Sweet Briar and the women who made it. (Kolowich)

This latter point is one worth emphasizing. The role of the tenured faculty is changing dramatically. On one hand, as I pointed out early in this volume, disruptive technologies have displaced the traditional full-time faculty from its central role in higher education. Consequently, the 65 percent of the faculty occupying tenured and tenure-track positions 40 years ago have been replaced by the 35 percent who now enjoy this privileged status.

That statistic is readily available and irrefutable. What is less apparent is how the fortunate third, who still cling to tenured appointments, are having to change their attitudes and their roles. No longer, below the level the Ivies and other wealthy R1 universities, can such faculty members get by teaching a three-plus-three (or lesser) academic-year workload and showing up on campus three (or fewer) days a week. Like Professor Thom-Kaley of Sweet Briar, such faculty are called upon to make meaningful—even crucial—contributions to recruitment and retention. Closing the deal is no longer exclusively the responsibility of the admissions office.

And why should it be? The tenured faculty are arguably the principal stakeholders in their institution, ironically at a time when their historic centrality to the delivery of instruction has waned. Most who are in their mid- or late-careers lack mobility, as other institutions prefer to fill coveted tenure-track openings with newly minted PhDs. For no other constituency in the college community—not even the students, who can usually transport most or all of their credits with alacrity—are the stakes higher.

But, if their teaching role is less than crucial, their unique ability to build mentor–mentee relationships with their students has the potential to move them back to the core of the business, provided they recognize and embrace the recruitment/retention challenge and own it.

In fact, I am arguing that for those students seeking a fuller college experience than can be found in an online program or a community college, the tenured faculty, if they choose, can create the value proposition in a way that no amount of campus amenities and extracurricular activities can do.

Building Vertical Relationships

If the advent of new teaching technologies on one hand and the demand for faculty participation in recruitment and retention on the other have blurred the lines between faculty and staff on the horizontal plane, relationships along the vertical continuum of American education also are shading one into the other. Four-year colleges are making themselves more affordable by accepting 60, and sometimes even more, credits from community colleges, thus enabling transfer students to average out the low (or nonexistent) tuition bills of their first two years with the pricier fees attached to their junior and senior years.

And an increasing number of four-year colleges are seeking to eliminate the "middle man" of the community college by dealing directly with local high schools. Others are part of a triumvirate that includes the local community college and offers the high school senior multiple paths to a degree and a career.

> Across the nation, dual enrollment—also called concurrent or joint enrollment—is growing in popularity. Its appeal taps into the widespread concerns about college costs as well as academic and career readiness. Such programs allow students to earn credits free or at a fraction of the cost that they would pay in college. The courses have also been shown to improve educational outcomes, like progress toward a degree. Some students apply general-education credits toward a degree from a participating four-year institution. Those interested in career and technical training can move directly into the work force after graduation or get a two-year degree much faster.
>
> Dual enrollment often helps institutions, too, by strengthening ties between colleges and their local high schools. Professors can shape how students are being prepared for college, while teachers gain professional-development opportunities and insights into what is expected of their students after graduation. (McMurtrie)

Here are those faculty members popping into the picture again. Bridging the gap between high school and college is an exercise that education faculty perform as a matter of course. Those engaged in training future K–12 teachers often spend much more of their workweeks in high and elementary schools, coordinating and supplementing student-teaching placements than they spend on their own college campuses. For other full-time faculty, the high-school corridor is *terra incognita*, unless and until they have secondary school children of their own. Beyond straightforward recruitment efforts, they now may find themselves teaching college-level courses in high school classrooms, providing a show-and-tell lesson while building those crucial teacher–student relationships that build the value proposition, while reducing the total cost of the student's ultimate goal, an affordable and attractive four-year degree.

After Bringing in the Students, We Still Need to Bring in the Bucks

So we—faculty and staff—have joined forces horizontally and built our vertical relationships—with high schools and community colleges—to create a value proposition sufficiently robust to attract the requisite student numbers to make ends meet. For us, the proposition only pays off when the tuition dollars come through our doors…and keep coming for the two, three, or four years the student attends until graduation.

Despite the best efforts of faculty and staff to retain matriculated students, the simple fact is that for the vast majority of private and (in this age of underfunding by many state legislatures) public universities, the inability of continuing students to afford tuition and fees remains the dominant reason given by those who drop or transfer out. In an effort to hang onto these students, schools must now engage in a delicate dance.

> When Tyson Cooper began working in student accounts 10 years ago, debt collection on college campuses was viewed as purely business and a "necessary evil," says the director of student financial services at the University of Southern Virginia.
>
> Today, with increased attention on student success and the long-term effects of unpaid accounts, institutions need to recognize the impact financial services staff have on recruitment and retention. It's a shift to thinking more about the big picture.
>
> Campus leaders increasingly consider the professionals who help students fulfill their financial commitments—mandatory for degree completion—as key partners, Cooper says. Yet collecting unpaid debt from students is by no means easy: Collectors must delicately try to preserve a student's positive relationship with the institution while ensuring the financial integrity of the enterprise. (Jackson)

In this article, *University Business* magazine offers six "smart practices":

(1) Establish a student-first culture
(2) Communicate policies clearly and in advance
(3) Be proactive
(4) Make it personal
(5) Offer payment plans
(6) Build campus-wide support

For the attentive reader, these practices should come as no surprise. As ever, it is the personal touch that wins the day, if it can be won. Indeed, *New York Times* columnist and best-selling prognosticator Thomas Friedman predicts in his latest tome that in our age of automation, robotics, and artificial intelligence, successful professional careers will be those that combine sophisticated technical skills with human-relations skill sets (Friedman). As with our tenured faculty, so too the denizens of the "back office," once engaged in "business as usual," must join the recruiting and retention team. Not only, as noted under Part A, above, must they be team mates in the negotiation to bring the student (and by implication her family) through the campus gates. They also must remain engaged in the team effort to keep matriculated students at the institution through to graduation…and ideally beyond the baccalaureate degree as continuing customers for master's degrees and even doctorates.

References

Clark University, "Overview," March 18, 2017, accessed at https://www.usnews.com/best-colleges/clark-university-massachusetts-2139

Education Advisory Board, "EAB Daily Briefing," December 1, 2015.

Fordham University, "Overview," March 18, 2017, accessed at https://www.usnews.com/best-colleges/fordham-university-2722

Friedman, Thomas L., *Thank You for Being Late: An Optimist's Guide to Thriving in the Age of Accelerations* (New York: Farrar, Straus and Giroux 2016).

Higher Education Consortium of Central Massachusetts (HECCMA), "For College Students," March 18, 2017, accessed at http://www.heccma.org/students/

Howard University, "Overview," March 18, 2017, accessed at https://www.usnews.com/best-colleges/howard-university-1448

Jackson, Nancy Mann, "Tuition: Past Due," *University Business*, April 2–17, at 47.

Kolowich, Steve, "How to Bring a College Back to Life," *Chronicle of Higher Education*, April 4, 2017.

Matthews, George J., Norman R. Smith and Bryan A. Carlson, *What College Trustees Need to Know* (Bloomington, IN: Universe 2013).

McGee, Jon, *The Changing Marketplace for Higher Education as a Commodity* (Baltimore, MD: Johns Hopkins University Press 2015).

McMurtrie, Beth, "How Colleges Are teaming Up With High Schools to Streamline Students' Paths," *Chronicle of Higher Education*, April 2, 2017.

Muhlenberg College, "The Real Deal on Financial Aid," March 18, 2017, accessed at http://www.muhlenberg.edu/main/admissions/therealdealonfinancialaid/

Selingo, Jeffrey J., "Colleges Heavily Discount Tuition, and It Might be a Race to Extinction," *Washington Post*, May 6, 2016, accessed at https://www.washingtonpost.com/news/grade-point/wp/2016/05/16/colleges-heavily-discount-tuition-and-it-might-be-a-race-to-extinction/?utm_term=.4334d64203c2, December 31, 2016.

Seltzer, Rick, "Discounting Hits New Highs," *Inside Higher Ed*, May 16, 2016, accessed at https://www.insidehighered.com/news/2016/05/16/discount-rates-rise-yet-again-private-colleges-and-universities, December 31, 2016.

University of San Francisco (USF), "Overview," March 18, 2017, accessed at https://www.usnews.com/best-colleges/university-san-francisco-1325

U.S. News (I), "A-Plus Schools for B Students," December 31, 2016, accessed at http://colleges.usnews.rankingsandreviews.com/best-colleges/rankings/national-universities/a-plus

U.S. News (II), "A-Plus Schools for B Students Methodology," December 31, 2016, accessed at http://www.usnews.com/education/best-colleges/articles/a-plus-schools-for-b-students-methodology

· 7 ·

ADDRESSING THE FACILITIES "ARMS RACE"

Herewith, a 2017 press release from central New Jersey's Rider University:

> Students attending Mercer County Community College can now experience campus life at Rider University as part of a new housing partnership between the two institutions.
>
> The formal agreement—one of several signed on Dec. 14 at a ceremony on Mercer's West Windsor campus—allows Mercer students to live in Rider's residence halls at a reduced rate. As campus residents, the students will have full access to the University's resources, including libraries, dining halls, and exercise and sports facilities. They will also be encouraged to participate in Rider's 150 student clubs and organizations, intramural sports and on-campus events, such as concerts, musicals, and Division I athletic events.
>
> "Rider University and Mercer County Community College have a long history in partnering for the common benefit of our students, and this innovative idea is an exciting new component of how we can help create successful university graduates," said Rider President Gregory G. Dell'Omo. "We look forward to sharing Rider's vibrant campus life with Mercer students."
>
> The housing agreement applies to both domestic and international students. For those who decide to continue their education at Rider toward a bachelor's degree, the University will offer tuition discounts in addition to the reduced housing rates.
>
> "This agreement is so important for those who could not otherwise take advantage of a college education," said MCCC President Dr. Jianping Wang. "Rider University is a shining example of a four-year institution with a dedication to serve. This could be a landmark arrangement others will follow."

Three new program-to-program agreements were also signed at the ceremony, strengthening the ties between Rider and Mercer and offering more opportunities for students seeking full junior-class admission to Rider after earning an associate degree at Mercer. The agreements guarantee transfer admission of Mercer students who complete an Associate of Arts in dance to Rider's Bachelor of Arts in dance performance; an Associate of Applied Science in advertising and graphic design to Rider's Bachelor of Arts in graphic design; and an Associate of Science to Rider's Bachelor of Science in Business Administration (accounting).

Mercer is Rider's largest articulation partner. The new agreements raise the total number of programs available to transfer between Rider and Mercer to 28, creating more educational opportunities than ever for Mercer students who want to complete their bachelor's degree.

"We are proud to continue our strong academic and educational partnership with Mercer," Dell'Omo said. "A collaboration like ours greatly benefits students as they move from community college to a four-year institution."

At the ceremony, Mercer and Rider also officially signed a guaranteed reverse credit transfer agreement. This allows students currently enrolled at Rider to complete the necessary credits toward an associate degree that would be awarded by Mercer.

In addition to presidents Dell'Omo and Wang, more than 30 faculty members and administrators from the two institutions attended the signing. (Grybowski)

As I pointed out in Chapter Six, breaking the vicious cycle of ever-rising tuition and ever-deepening tuition discounts requires colleges and universities, especially private nonprofits, to partner with high schools and community colleges in averaging out college costs by giving students a head start on their four-year degrees. Rider's renting of empty beds to Mercer students is a natural corollary to accepting 60 (or even more) AP and community college transfer credits.

A residence-hall arrangement such as this is hardly the ideal for the four-year institution. Just as the university would prefer to admit freshmen for a full four years, it would prefer to fill its beds with its own students. But in today's campus-eat-campus world, this arrangement is a palatable second-best solution to diminished enrollments at the four-year school and a lack of funding to build dorms on the community college side of the deal.

The community college partnership is certainly not the most innovative relationship being pursued by four-year colleges in this Fifth-Wave era. Schools are also joint venturing with for-profit developers. As we saw in Chapter Three, some states, such as New Jersey, have embraced public–private partnerships as a significant tool to leverage public funding for the revitalization of their college campuses. An increasing number of private colleges are following suit.

For example, New York's St. Joseph's College with campuses in Brooklyn and on Long Island needed to build student housing to remain competitive. As its leadership set about addressing this demand, it confronted two challenges: a lack of appetite among potential donors for funding dorms and a $26 million debt burden that made borrowing difficult, if not impossible. The solution? St. Joe's partnered with a private developer to build a $30 million, 300-bed residence hall on its Patchogue (L.I.) campus (Gardner).

"Private financing deals for student housing have become fairly common at big public institutions. The University of Kentucky, for one prominent example, is in the middle of a $442-million, privately financed student-housing revamp that will bring more than 6,000 new beds to its campus.

"Until about five years ago, however, few colleges the size of St. Joseph's—total student enrollment under 4,000—would have allowed a company to have a financial stake in their campus and in their operations" (Gardner).

As enrollments have declined, as discounts have deepened, and as budgets have tightened, outmoded residence facilities have been an albatross, if not a millstone, around such small institutions' necks. In my day—aka the Sixties—one large bathroom facility shared by an entire floor, fans rather than air conditioners, and cramped quarters were all part of the "dorm" experience. For freshmen, this was part of the rite of passage from high school to college. Upper-classmen, who chose to remain in the residence halls as opposed to a frat house or apartment, might trade up to a four-student suite with some amenities or maybe not. Just as often, the "step up" was to a hall featuring somewhat larger rooms, or possibly singles, but little else by way of improvement.

In our Fifth-Wave era, students expect better, much better. And small schools simply can't meet the competition head-on on their own. Observed James A. Kadamus, vice president of Sightlines, a facilities-consulting company, "[M]any small colleges [are] saying, 'If we don't build those kinds of facilities, we're not going to attract students'" (Gardner).

Sightlines' menu of services is a blueprint of what ought to be done to join this trend:

- Facilities Benchmarking and Analysis: Sightlines contends, "On average, campus facilities are worth four to five times the value of endowments." Do you have the tool kit required to manage your largest asset, the firm asks? The first such tool that ought to be in the kit, argues the consulting company, is a holistic assessment of the campus(es). From this assessment should emerge a strategic plan. From a such a plan should then emerge a dialogue about:

(1) Securing funding to tackle deferred maintenance;
(2) An understanding of realistic investment levels;
(3) Developing a "facilities story" to tell to key stakeholders;
(4) Creating facilities targets that align with the institutional mission and vision. (Sightlines)

- Capital Planning: Once you have tallied up your facility assets and needs, and having incorporated this analysis into your institution's strategic plan, the next step is to create a capitalization plan that will move the current campus from status quo to vision. "Capital programs on a university campus need clearly defined processes for identifying, selecting, approving, and executing project investments. The process needs to differentiate repairs from modernization and alteration projects, while simultaneously aligning investments to complement campus programmatic goals. The process must align investment needs to financial capacity and clearly explain the rationale for project deferral—an explanation that focuses on sequencing and timing of investments rather than selecting 'winners and losers' of funding." The components of such a capital-planning process should include:
(1) Inclusiveness—All key constituencies should be heard;
(2) Credibility—Comprehensiveness and integration are the two attributes of a plan that will appear credible to donors and investors;
(3) Flexibility—In addition to modifying preliminary plans to reflect input of key constituents, including alumni and students, you must be prepared to make midstream modifications in the face of changed circumstances, which may arise;
(4) Affordability—Enhancing not only credibility with donors, investors, and other constituents, affordability helps ensure survival in the face of unanticipated short-term adversities;
(5) Sustainability—The plan must be compatible with the managerial capabilities of your institution (Sightline).
- Space Management: When still "wet behind the ears," in 1974, I directed the PR office of Case Western Reserve University. The CWRU had been created in 1968 by the merger of Case Institute of Technology and Western Reserve University, two venerable, respected institutions, which had coexisted along Euclid Avenue in Cleveland (OH) for a century or more. During the Vietnam War, when tens of thousands of young men became full-time college students for the deferments such

status brought from being drafted into the military, enrollments had burgeoned. Case was no exception. Furthermore, the Department of Housing and Urban Development had ponied up federal funding in the form of loans to help universities meet the housing demand this influx generated. The upshot was that many a school, Case included, had overbuilt dorm facilities. When the draft lottery replaced the deferment system, and then when the war finally ended, many male students dropped out of school. Concurrently, Cleveland State University and Cuyahoga Community College had come on the Cleveland college scene to compete for a diminished pool of prospective applicants. The upshot: CWRU absorbed a few years of multimillion-dollar operating deficits en route to adjusting to these changed circumstances. Case, a major R1 institution, had the endowment and research income to absorb these budgetary shortfalls. Today's small, tuition-driven colleges have no such cushions. Consequently, it is crucial that use of existing facilities be maximized before new ones are constructed.

According to Sightlines, classrooms as an example are occupied less than 60 percent of the available time. At Rider University, where I have spent more than two decades, the VP for Institutional Analysis led an early 2000s study, which identified all available classroom facilities and developed a computerized plan—called affectionately "the brick wall"—to ensure that all such spaces were either accommodating classes or dedicated to alternative purposes throughout the business day and, so far as possible, into the evening hours.

So, let's assume your institution has engaged in the planning process prescribed by Sightlines. And let's make the further assumption that your management team has identified new dorms as a priority project... crucial to attracting the students your tuition-driven institution desperately needs, but beyond the reach of your strapped finances? What does a joint venture with a for-profit firm look like?

Let's circle back to New York's St. Joe's College, which partnered with an outfit called Mosaic Capital Group. The Patchogue campus had been run as a commuter college due to the lack of residence halls. Benchmarking and analysis indicated a 300-bed dormitory could be filled, if price and amenities met customer expectations. To minimize risk and up-front carrying costs, the parties agreed to a phased project. The 200 beds of the first phase, if successfully filled, will produce profits capable of helping fund phase two. If an occupancy shortfall occurs, both parties' exposure will be limited (Gardener).

And what of other new facilities? Athletic, science & technology, and arts/entertainment facilities are more appealing than dorms with alumni, trustees, and other donors seeking "naming opportunities." Key to attracting the big bucks is making a marriage between the potential donor and the desired facility. To wit:

> Rider breaks ground for Jason Thompson Court
> The groundbreaking is the latest phase of a multiphased project to enhance and expand Rider's historic Alumni Gymnasium
> By
> Rider Sports Information
> 07/28/2015
>
> Less than a decade ago Jason Thompson of the Golden State Warriors was making a name for himself on the Rider University basketball court.
> Now, Rider is making a basketball court with Jason Thompson's name on it.
> Groundbreaking took place Monday on construction of an 8,400 square foot basketball practice facility, the second phase of a multi-phased project to enhance and expand Rider's historic Alumni Gymnasium, the oldest building on Rider's Lawrenceville campus. Construction is expected to be completed in spring 2016.
> On hand to help with the groundbreaking was Thompson, a 2008 Rider graduate, seven-year veteran of the National Basketball Association and one of the newest members of the defending NBA champions Golden State Warriors. Thompson's generous contribution to the project led to the naming of the basketball court in the new facility in his honor.
> "Jason has always been a great ambassador for Rider University, both during his time at Rider and his time following graduation in the NBA," said Rider Director of Athletics Don Harnum. "The Jason Thompson Court recognizes Jason for his financial commitment to the Campaign for Rider Athletics, his passion for Rider Basketball and his willingness to help us move the program forward."
> "I had a great experience as a student and as a player during my time at Rider," said Thompson, an All-American who graduated from Rider with a degree in Communication, along with 2,040 points and a program-record 1,171 rebounds in 122 games. "The people at Rider did a lot for me to help me get where I am today and I am fortunate to be in a position to contribute to a project that will help elevate the profile of the basketball program and the University."
> Thompson played in 541 NBA games as a Sacramento King, after being the 12th player (and first college graduate) selected in the 2008 NBA draft. Thompson has compiled over 5,000 points and 3,750 rebounds in seven seasons in the NBA, all for the Kings.
> The first phase of the multi-phased project, completed two years ago, included the addition of a state-of-the-art HD video board; modern heating, air conditioning and lighting; new flooring; a new sound system and branding initiatives.

"The completion of the first phase gave Alumni Gym a much-needed updated look and feel," Harnum said.

The Alumni Gym Campaign is funded entirely through the generous support of private donations. "I'd like to thank our campaign leadership team and all our donors who have supported this important project. It will dramatically enhance the daily lives of our student-athletes and coaches, bolster recruiting and afford us greater scheduling flexibility for basketball, volleyball, and wrestling, which compete in Alumni Gym," Harnum said.

Future phases of the Alumni Gym Campaign will include expanded seating capacity with additional premium seats, enhanced fan amenities, renovated locker rooms and office space, and a strength and conditioning center. (Rider Sports Information)

Attracting a significant corporate contribution may require something more than a "match made in heaven." Potential real-dollar value may be a necessary component. Mere mention of this causes some academics to bridle. Stories of undue influence of self-interested corporations upon academic research projects they have funded echoes down the hallowed halls of our ivory towers. However, arrangements that fall somewhere on the spectrum between the joint-ventures involving private financiers and developers in the residence hall arena and the outright gifts exemplified by NBA star Jason Thompson's gift to his alma mater, are possible within the bounds of academic research integrity. Often, too, public funds—federal and//or state—are implicated in such undertakings.

So far as facilities are concerned, several models can be identified. The first, involving no new fund-raising or construction by the participating university, involves exporting the delivery of instruction to the existing physical facilities of the partner corporation. For example:

Boeing and University of Washington

On December 4, The Boeing Company took another step in its transition from metal to composite structures. Addressing the critical training challenge posed by aircraft composites, the materials used to build the 787 Dreamliner, it honored more than 80 engineers and technical professionals at a graduation ceremony for the University of Washington-Boeing Certificate Programs in Composite Materials and Modern Aircraft Structures.

Boeing also celebrated its corporate-university educational partnership with the UW, which it has called vital to the future of the 787 and development of other next-generation aircraft. In fact, Boeing officials have hailed the partnership as a new kind of corporate training model, one that is applicable far beyond the aerospace industry.

Tailored to Boeing requirements, these programs are co-developed by Boeing's Learning, Training and Development (LTD) unit and the University of Washington.

"This partnership represents a new mode of collaboration between industry and academia, one that blends the academic rigor expected from the University of Washington with the practical applications that are critical to Boeing and its partner companies," said Michael Richey of Boeing LTD.

Jon Schneider, Director of Boeing LTD-Engineering, has said of the program, "This is a model that can be leveraged across industry and higher education. When educational partnerships change the way something is done or created, they create a competitive value."

Since the inception of UW-Boeing Certificate Programs in 2005, a total of 330 Boeing employees have earned certificates in one or more of the trio of composites programs offered. To quantify the benefit to Boeing of its educational partnership with the UW, a study by Boeing LTD has calculated the return on investment of one of the programs at more than 500 percent.

Jose Ramos, Boeing Chief Engineer, Stress Analysis and Technology Support, said the composites certificate program provides tremendous value. "It really has let us educate people in a technology that wasn't well understood by a large portion of our population. It's improving the technical capabilities of structures engineers not only on the 787 but on other programs as well."

The UW-Boeing corporate education model is remarkable for its depth of collaboration between industry and academia. Taught onsite at Boeing facilities by UW faculty, Boeing subject matter experts, and leading professionals from the FAA, courses are tailored to blend theoretical fundamentals with the practical applications critical to Boeing. These include hands-on lab and design components. Students can take what they learn in the classroom at night and apply it on the job the next day. (Boeing)

Another model is exemplified by the Yale Entrepreneurial Institute. Though hardly hard-pressed for funds, the New England Ivy supports the institute's facilities by offering memberships to for-profit participants. For example:

> *Center for Engineering Innovation and Design*: Membership with the Center for Engineering Innovation and Design (CEID) grants access to innovating equipment and technology like laser cutters, 3D printers, and machine shops. Members can sign up for special and recurring workshops and training sessions that take place in the CEID. *Highlights include*: Workshops, Makerbot Training, Laser Cutter Training, Machine Shop Training, CEID Wednesday Night Event Series, Hackathons, and the CEID Summer Fellowship. (Yale Entrepreneurial Institute)

Another example is drawn from yet another Ivy, the University of Pennsylvania:

The Nano-Bio probe facility is a unique lab that serves as an incubator for new probes of nanostructure behavior and associated instrumentation development. It is equipped with a suite of nine advanced scanning probe systems, opto-electronic transport tools, and optical probes operating in fluid, ambient, or vacuum environments. The Facility is currently used by approximately 100 investigators from within Penn, industry labs, and educational programs. (Penn Engineering)

At the other end of the spectrum are full-blown partnerships, such as this one at the University of Delaware:

The University of Delaware's Science, Technology and Advanced Research (STAR) Campus is located just a half mile from the heart of UD's primary academic campus.

STAR is already home to:
- A performance computing company named by Forbes as one of America's Most Promising Companies
- A manufacturer of clean fuel-cell power sources whose energy servers provide power to Fortune 500 clients including Google, Wal-Mart, AT&T, and Coca-Cola.
- A test zero-emissions vehicle laboratory supported by the U.S. Department of Energy, the State of Delaware, NRG Energy, Honda, and BMW.
- UD's Health Sciences Complex of classrooms, research laboratories, and open-to-the-public care clinics. Operating under the name STAR Health, UD's comprehensive clinics offer major health and prevention services including: primary care, therapy, speech, mental health services, care coordination, nutrition counseling, fitness counseling, and health coaching.
    - o Local residents can access high-quality care and work directly with researchers developing advanced ways to treat illnesses and injuries.
    - o UD students train to become the next generation of healthcare practitioners in the clinics, including one belonging to the world-class physical therapy department, a program ranked #1 by U.S. News and World Report.
- A 10,000 square-foot wet lab that will serve as an incubator for small research companies (University of Delaware).

As this book went off to press, the University of Delaware and its for-profit partner were about to join in developing a hotel for the STAR campus.

The University of Delaware and 1743 Holdings, LLC, are seeking Letters of Interest from potential partners with the demonstrated financial, development and operational expertise to bring a full-service hotel to the [STAR] Campus, located on 272 acres of land approximately ¼ mile from the University's Main Campus in Newark, Delaware. (University of Delaware II)

U of D's STAR Campus brings all of the above together. Here, we have an example of a public university partnering across scientific and technological research, technology transfer to private industry, combined with housing facilities and retail amenities…all synthesized in a single campus.

References

Boeing Corporation, "Boeing and University of Washington," April 23, 2017, accessed at http://seattle.sawe.org/archives/31

Gardner, Lee, "Small Colleges Risk a Turn to Private Capital to Build Housing," *Chronicle of Higher Education*, February 25, 2016.

Grybowski, Adam, "Innovative Partnership Allows Mercer County College students to live on Rider University Campus," December 16, 2016, accessed at http://www.rider.edu/news/2016/12/16/innovative-partnership-allows-mercer-county-college-students-live-rider-university-campus (reprinted with permission).

Penn Engineering, "Labs and Facilities," April 24, 2017, accessed at http://www.seas.upenn.edu/research/labs-facilities.php

Rider Sports Information, "Rider Breaks ground for Jason Thompson Court," July 28, 2015, accessed at http://www.rider.edu/news/2015/10/30/rider-breaks-ground-jason-thompson-court (reprinted with permission), April 23, 2017.

Sightlines, April 23, 2017, accessed at http://www.sightlines.com

University of Delaware, "STAR Campus," April 24, 2017, accesses at http://www1.udel.edu/star/

University of Delaware II, "Invitation to Submit Letters of Interest…", April 24, 2017, accessed at http://www1.udel.edu/star/downloads/invitation-to-submit-letters-STAR-hotel.pdf

Yale Entrepreneurial Institute, "Campus Innovation Centers," April 24, 2017, accessed at http://yei.yale.edu/campus-innovation-centers-0

· 8 ·

CAPITALIZING ON A POTENTIAL WINDOW OF REGULATORY RELIEF

Enter the Trump Administration

I concluded Chapter Four with the observation that, under billionaire Betsy DeVos, the U.S. Department of Education can be expected to relax its regulatory grip on our industry. In Chapter Five, I outlined the dimensions of the regulatory burden weighing down the already-beleaguered nonprofit sector. Again, I suggested that some relief may be in the offing. Here, permit me to expand that prognostication to include the entire federal bureaucracy. How so? Let's begin with one of President Donald Trump's first executive orders.

EXECUTIVE ORDER

- - - - - - -

REDUCING REGULATION AND CONTROLLING REGULATORY COSTS

By the authority vested in me as President by the Constitution and the laws of the United States of America, including the Budget and Accounting Act of 1921, as amended (31 U.S.C. 1101 et seq.), section 1105 of title 31, United States Code, and section 301 of title 3, United States Code, it is hereby ordered as follows:

Section 1. Purpose. It is the policy of the executive branch to be prudent and financially responsible in the expenditure of funds, from both public and private sources. In addition to the management of the direct expenditure of taxpayer dollars through

the budgeting process, it is essential to manage the costs associated with the governmental imposition of private expenditures required to comply with Federal regulations. Toward that end, it is important that for every one new regulation issued, at least two prior regulations be identified for elimination, and that the cost of planned regulations be prudently managed and controlled through a budgeting process.
Sec. 2. Regulatory Cap for Fiscal Year 2017. (a) Unless prohibited by law, whenever an executive department or agency (agency) publicly proposes for notice and comment or otherwise promulgates a new regulation, it shall identify at least two existing regulations to be repealed. (Presidential Executive Order)

Many of us in higher education might not very much like Mr. Trump or his Secretary of Education. We may rightly worry about their plans for student-loan funding and other targets of the Administration's proposed budgetary cuts. And we may chafe under the tightened restrictions on the mobility of our international and undocumented students.

But…when regulatory compliance accounts for as much as 11 percent of many colleges' budgets and as much as 15 percent of staff time (Moran)—we should give the devil his due.

So…if we can agree that fewer regulations may save us significant money in this time of financial stress, the next question might be, what has happened so far ("so far" being mid-2017)? Let's begin with teacher education.

Teacher-Preparation Evaluation

Among the 11th-hour rules and regs released by the Obama Administration in the autumn of 2016 were rules intended to force states to rate teacher-preparation programs on a range of criteria, including the number of grads who take jobs in "high-need schools," how long alumni stay in the teaching profession, and how effectively these graduates impact student-learning outcomes (Iasevoll).

If, as I argue in this book, higher education is being buffeted by a "perfect storm" in this Fifth-Wave era, the same may accurately be said about public K–12 education. As much by Secretary DeVos, a vocal proponent and generous supporter of charter schools, as anyone, public schools have been criticized for poor performance. Simultaneously in many states, public school teachers and their unions have seen their collective-bargaining rights curbed or curtailed; underfunded pension plans and rich health care benefits, enshrined in collective bargaining, likewise have been under scrutiny and, sometimes, attack. So too is tenure in many jurisdictions. Last, but not least, the federal

"No Child Left Behind" law, a Bush-era legacy, has helped turn K–12 teaching into K–12 testing. Little wonder, then, that fewer college students are choosing careers in K–12 teaching and alumni are leaving the profession in unprecedented numbers.

> Several big states have seen alarming drops in enrollment at teacher training programs. The numbers are grim among some of the nation's largest producers of new teachers: In California, enrollment is down 53 percent over the past five years. It's down sharply in New York and Texas as well. (Westervelt)

Meanwhile, some states have been ratcheting up the requirements for teacher certification. For example, beginning in academic year 2018–2019, student teachers in New Jersey will be required to complete an additional 175 hours of clinical experience. At least 100 of those hours must come in the semester immediately prior to a senior's spring full-time student-teaching experience (Clark). These same Garden State college students are required to complete a second major in a liberal art or science. They must pass a series of Praxis exams. And they must maintain a 3.5 GPA.

Accreditation requirements for our schools and colleges of education are also onerous. In 2015, the Association of Colleges for Teacher Education, the organization representing teachers' colleges, criticized the leading accrediting body, the Council for the Accreditation of Educator Preparation, saying "Specific concerns are related to the accreditation standards, process for accreditation, costs associated with accreditation…" (Sawchuck). More about this immediately below.

Bottom line: If any area of our programmatic offerings requires regulatory relief, it is teacher education. In the first days of the Trump Administration, that relief was forthcoming. Reversing those 11th-hour Obama regulations is woefully insufficient to staunch the bleeding of teachers from our nation's public schools. But it is a start.

What about regulation more broadly? Will the Trump Administration take on the accreditation establishment? (I think it should.)

Whither Accreditation?

In Chapter Four, I noted the gutting of the for-profit sector's major accrediting agency by the U.S. Department of Education…again, an 11th-hour Obama Administration move. Above, in this chapter, I've cited to criticism of CAEP, the major accreditor of our teacher-preparation programs. This latter critique mentioned cost as a concern. Cost in fact is no small concern. A 2015 study by Vanderbilt University and the Boston Consulting Group concluded that regional accreditation alone costs higher education $3 billion per year. Add to this $3 billion more for programmatic accreditations, such as CAEP and business schools' AACSB, among the many (Stratford).

Can we crawl out from under this accreditation conundrum? A movement may be afoot to do just that. "Accrediting agencies are facing intense scrutiny from academics, policy makers and the public, with the latest salvo being the decision by Northwestern University's school of journalism and communications to ditch its accreditor" (Fain).

Important to clarify here is the distinction between regional and programmatic accreditation. As Northwestern's move implies, programmatic accreditors lend a seal of approval to university programs, which presumably helps recruitment of students. (Northwestern's journalism school is sufficiently prestigious to prosper without such a seal.) By contrast, regional accreditors (such as SACS, which played a major part in the Hiwassee College story in Chapter Five) and the now-defunct for-profit accreditor mentioned in Chapter Four, are gatekeepers to the federal student-aid cornucopia. While programmatic accreditors can be dumped by schools and colleges enjoying a free-standing reputation sufficient to attract sufficient students, the regional accreditors are a different "kettle of fish." They generally are viewed by most higher ed administrators as the lesser of two evils. We usually view the dreaded alternative to be direct oversight by the U.S. Department of Education.

Might the Trump Administration relax or eliminate such oversight? The answer, as of mid-2017, remains a cipher. In May 2017, the DeVos DOE finalized its decision to terminate recognition of the Accrediting Council for Independent Colleges and Schools. The department filed a brief supporting the Obama Administration's move in a lawsuit filed by the ACICS. Meanwhile most of the 245 for-profit schools affected by the DOE's action have applied to the Accrediting Commission of Career Schools and Colleges (Fain II).

Those who expected the Trump/DeVos regime to provide swift relief to the beleaguered for-profit sector no doubt are disappointed by its decision. The rest of us, who are accredited by SACS and its other regional counterparts, are left to guess whither the Trump Administration will take regional accreditation. The Trump/DeVos DOE may yet decide to cause all regional accreditors to go the way of the ACICS. If that were to occur, I doubt that

CAPITALIZING ON A POTENTIAL WINDOW OF REGULATORY RELIEF 115

many reading these words would see this as a leap from the frying pan into the fire. Perhaps better the devil we know?

For now, opportunities to reduce accreditation costs lie with the movement to drop programmatic accreditors. Factors to be considered include:

- Will eliminating a programmatic accreditor have a material impact on your school's operating budget? Will it materially free-up staff and faculty time for student recruiting, retention, and the like?
- Is the currently accredited program reputationally and academically robust enough to sustain its enrollment postaccreditor-dump?

This is the trade-off that requires careful evaluation, before joining the Northwesterns of our industry. But such an evaluation (or re-evaluation) may be well worth the exercise.

Let's examine just one case on point: AACSB. Here's what the organization says of itself:

> As the world's largest business education alliance, AACSB International—The Association to Advance Collegiate Schools of Business (AACSB) connects educators, students, and business to achieve a common goal: to create the next generation of great leaders. Synonymous with the highest standards of excellence since 1916, AACSB provides quality assurance, business education intelligence, and professional development services to over 1,500 member organizations and more than 785 accredited business schools worldwide. With its global headquarters in Tampa, Florida, USA; Europe, Middle East, and Africa headquarters in Amsterdam, the Netherlands; and Asia Pacific headquarters in Singapore, AACSB's mission is to foster engagement, accelerate innovation, and amplify impact in business education. (AACSB)

As I did earlier in this book, I am fond of paraphrasing the lyrics of Gilbert and Sullivan's operetta "The Gondoliers": When everybody's somebody, then no one's anybody. AACSB is a case on point in my opinion.

Obtaining an exact number of business schools in the United States is tougher than you might think…try it. However, one source lists 395 such schools. Of these, this same source lists only 65 that lack AACSB accreditation, i.e., about 16 percent. And, of that 16 percent, about 10 percent hold alternative accreditations, driving the percentage of unaccredited schools below 14 percent (Wikipedia). It's difficult to claim that AACSB accreditation gives a school a distinct advantage over the competition, when nearly all competitors also are AACSB accredited.

In fact, other rankings appear to be far more distinctive, e.g., *U.S. News & World Report's* "Best Business Schools" (U.S. News).

However, it's possible that a corollary to the Gilbert and Sullivan song pertains: if everybody's somebody, you can't afford to be a nobody. Some researchers assert that this is precisely the strategy behind AACSB's tactics.

> The workload at some AACSB-accredited colleges is nine credits of teaching a year and at others it is 21 credits. How can this be? The reason for this is that AACSB attempts to determine whether a business program meets the mission the college has established for itself. Yes, every school decides on its own mission. This means that each of the AACSB-accredited colleges and universities may have very different goals and standards in terms of research and teaching quality. This statement about AACSB accreditation from Bob Reid explains how the process works:
>
> Bob Reid, AACSB's chief accreditation officer and a former dean at James Madison University's business school, says the group now assesses schools in the context of their individual missions, rather than against a common standard....
>
> One reason AACSB adopted a mission-based approach was to meet a perceived threat from other accrediting bodies (citations omitted). This enables AACSB to enlarge the number of AACSB-accredited schools and earn more in fees. According to Korn (2013), in fiscal 2011, AACSB earned more than $5 million in accreditation fees, $3.2 million in dues, and additional revenues from attendance at annual conferences and seminars. (Friedman and Kass-Schraibman, p. 2)

Bottom line: "Unfortunately, the list of AACSB-accredited schools is slowly morphing into something that resembles a regional higher education accreditor such as the Middle States Association of Colleges and Schools" (Friedman and Kass-Schraibman, p. 1). Then, why do it? "The Dean at Georgetown University's School of Business, David Thomas, stated: 'The presence of accreditation doesn't differentiate you [as an elite school], but the absence of it does cause more noise and questions'" (Friedman and Kass-Schraibman, p. 2).

Of greater concern in the context of this book,

> Moreover, pursuing AACSB accreditation may be a disaster for a college that has serious problems that include decaying and decrepit infrastructure with health and safety problems, primitive classrooms, mushrooming class sizes, and administrative bloat. If AACSB is being used as a way for a college president or provost to brag that their school has achieved this "prestigious" accomplishment, it may cause more harm than good. The cost of achieving AACSB accreditation can be as high as $10 million or more. Spending scarce funds on accreditation and ignoring the infrastructure is not a wise move. (Friedman and Kass-Schraibman, p. 3)

Consequently, as we saw with Northwestern University's journalism school,

> Queens College of the City University of New York (CUNY) decided that the millions it would cost to achieve AACSB accreditation was not worth it given that money was needed for other purposes. Queens College has an excellent reputation and its college ranking according to US News & World Report is #38 among Regional Universities North with an overall score of 64/100. (Friedman and Kass-Schraibman, p. 3)

Meanwhile, "a 2015 list of 'America's 32 Worst Colleges' includes eight in the bottom 10 that have AACSB accreditation" (Friedman and Kass-Schraibman, p. 4). And the list of accredited schools keeps growing, as the organization continually globalizes its accreditation activities.

Let me be clear: My purpose is not to "bad rap" AACSB. However, its history makes for a good example of why, as I noted earlier in this section, accrediting organizations are under fire, and why—as we strive to ride the Fifth Wave, regulatory relief in this key-expense category may be welcome.

The AACSB's forays onto the global stage also make for a natural segue into a consideration of regulation of the international-student segment of our business models.

Managing Our International Students

During the first six months of the Trump Presidency, our attention was focused on his two ill-fated executive orders aimed at restricting travel from a group of predominantly Muslim nations. The administration's anti-immigrant policies sewed panic in the undocumented-alien communities across the country. Under the guidance of one of Mr. Trump's several appointees from the ranks of the military, Homeland Security heightened its enforcement activities. Discussion of the wall along America's southern border intensified, even if actual construction did not. Much was made by the media of illegal immigrants leaving the States for Canada. The capper was Trump's "Dreamers" order recission.

In the midst of all this law-enforcement, litigation, and media controversy, a number of universities—some quite prominent—declared themselves to be "sanctuary campuses," meaning they would not voluntarily cooperate with ICE agents seeking to arrest undocumented students.

Lost amidst all this "noise" was the issue of managing our international students.

In the wake of 9/11, more than a decade and a half ago, the newly organized Department of Homeland Security created the Student and Exchange Visitor Program (SEVP). Here's how it works.

Students from foreign countries typically obtain one of two types of visas in order to attend American colleges and universities: the F-1 visa or the J-1 visa. The first of these is intended for students who intend to spend multiple years in the states and earn their degrees from U.S. institutions. F-1 visas are administered by the US Citizenship and Immigration Service, one of two agencies spawned from the INS and located in the Department of Homeland Security after 9/11. The J-1 is a broad umbrella of a visa, administered by the U.S. Department of State and covering all manner of visiting scholars, including exchange students attending U.S. schools for a semester or a year of study, before returning home to complete their degrees.

Prior to September 11, 2001, universities issued the Form I-20 as a multiple-page, carbon-paper form to international applicants along with their offers of admission. The would-be students then took the form to their local U.S. embassy or consulate, where they were interviewed, and (ideally) issued an F-1 visa. Once the visa was issued, it was anybody's guess what became of the student, if s/he failed to show up on campus. Once the F-1 visa holder stepped off a plane and passed through customs at a U.S. airport, s/he could melt into the crowd, never to be seen again. The host university had no obligation to report the "no show." And the INS never followed up.

Among those foreigners who entered the United States on an F-1 visa was a 9/11 hijacker. This fact is of no practical significance. Most of the others entered with equivalent ease on tourist visas and the majority were able to obtain state-issued drivers licenses (FAIR). However, an "urban legend" has sprouted and bloomed to the effect that numerous members of the 9/11 terrorist group entered on student visas (Annenburg).

At the heart of the SEVP is the Student and Exchange Visitor Information System (SEVIS). Although instigated by an exaggerated impression of the role student visas played in the 9/11 attacks, SEVP was a good idea. Colleges and universities were required to apply for SEVIS status. They were vetted by officers and contractors in the employment of the US Immigration Control and Enforcement (ICE) agency, the second descendant of the ineffectual INS.

The SEVIS is an online system accessed by Designated School Officials, who have been individually vetted and trained, and whose passwords must be changed every few months. The Form I-10 is created online, then printed, and signed by a DSO (who may be an admissions official at the university in the first instance). When the applicant presents herself at the U.S. consulate, the consular officer conducting her interview can confirm the validity of the form online. Once the F-1 visa is issued, the applicant must present herself at the host institution's international-student office within 60 days or the visa will automatically be cancelled. Additionally, the student must report for reaffirmation by the same campus office shortly after the start of every subsequent semester. The SEVIS also handles the State Department's J-1 visas in much the same fashion. The SEVIS also manages student internships, and postgraduation employment in the U.S. Universities must apply for recertification every two years.

Just as SEVP was created at least in part out of a mistaken impression of the relationship between F-1 visas and the 9/11 attacks, the system arguably sustains a false sense of security. Here's why:

> The Department of Homeland Security has lost track of more than 6,000 foreign nationals who entered the United States on student visas, overstayed their welcome, and essentially vanished—exploiting a security gap that was supposed to be fixed after the Sept. 11, 2001 terror attacks. (ABC News)

When ABC News reported this story in late 2014, it learned that 58,000 foreign students had overstayed their visas. The 6,000 in the story's lead were the ones classified as of "heightened concern." The vanished students weren't the sole concern raised by the news report.

One school on the approved list, MicroPower Career Institute, licensed by the state of New York, continued to have four campuses on the approved list, even though five of the school's top officials—including its president—were indicted on charges of visa fraud in May. According to the indictment, 80 percent of the foreign students enrolled in MicroPower had delinquent attendance, putting them out of compliance with their visas. But the school did not report them, the indictment said. All five school officials pleaded not guilty in the case (ABC News).

Have things improved in the succeeding years? Not to my knowledge.

So, what should we conclude? Well, one plausible conclusion is that a significant increase in federal regulatory control over U.S. colleges and universities has failed to result in a concomitant increase in national security. Like the Transportation Safety Administration's Herculean efforts at out airports, which regularly fail infiltration tests (Bradner and Marsh), but continue to make our lives miserable in endless security lines, SEVP adds to the regulatory burden on college campuses without solving the perceived problem.

And, yet, this is a rare area in which the Trump Administration wants more, not less, regulatory activity. What's a college or university to do?

Worth consideration are third-party services, which can manage your foreign students for you, while cutting your costs and even enhancing your income. Here are some examples:

- *Ellucian International Student and Scholar Management:* Ellucian is known for its recruitment and retention software solutions (Ellucian). The international-student division purports to provide a comprehensive, SEVIS-compliant tracking system, which also claims to contribute to student retention. An administrative endorsement on the home page reads, "Ellucian International Student & Scholar Management helps us keep track of what is happening with our international enrollment and programs. We can see how many students transferred and why; how many didn't complete their programs and why" (Ellucian International).
- *Kings Education:* If you have a small international-student population, you may object that services such as offered by Ellucian are economical only if the numbers of such students are substantial. Programs like Kings Education may offer a worthy alternative. Kings partners with U.S. colleges and universities, including my own institution. "Rider University has partnered with Kings Education to offer English as a second language instruction on our Lawrenceville Campus. Language students will reside on campus and have access to all our facilities" (Rider). How does such a partnership contribute to the profitability of our international-student operation, while providing regulatory relief? Several ways: Kings recruits international students and brings them to campus; Kings may also manage the initial SEVIS registration, depending upon the partnership agreement; the host institution is compensated by Kings for the facilities used by the ESL operation, which typically includes room and board services; and, most important, students completing the ESL program often matriculate to the host institution.

These steps may help. Beyond them requires educating the Trump White House and the DeVos DOE on the importance of international students to the U.S. economy. In a typical academic year, a million students are studying in the United States from all over the world (IIE). This is an enormous piece of global business running contrary to the general trend of trade deficits that Mr. Trump says he wants to bring back into balance. Instead, his visa and immigration policies are precipitating hostility toward international students and making them uncomfortable about coming to study in America (WBUR).

As I implied in Chapter One, the global ("flat earth") marketplace—so devastating to American manufacturing—may be the ultimate salvation of American higher education. With only 1 percent of the human population possessing college degrees and American higher education still the best in the world, Trump and company should be made to perceive that we present the best opportunity for job creation and economic growth in the nation.

President Trump and his advisors, especially Secretary DeVos, must be made to understand that the regulatory window needs to be opened wider, not slammed shut, if we in higher education are going to build on our substantial base of international customers, rather than watching helplessly as it erodes. Post-9/11 regulation, ala SEVIS, has already weighed us down with little apparent impact on national security.

Meanwhile, Canada is eating our lunch.

> With the two most popular destinations for international students, the United States and Britain, tarnished by rising isolationist and antiforeigner sentiment, Canada, with its reputation for openness and safety, appears to be the main beneficiary. Universities across the country report record-setting applications from overseas, and international enrollments this fall are also expected to soar. (Fischer)

The Trump Administration can easily cure this problem, if it recognizes and addresses it before the 2017–2018 academic-year slump becomes an international-student pattern.

What Else Can the Trump Administration Do?

Almost any regulatory relief is welcome, as I have suggested above.

But doesn't the government have an interest in, even an obligation to, protect the consumer? And the taxpayer, too, meaning the taxpayer's money that goes to student loans and the like? Yes, indeed, it does. However, this just might be an instance in which the free market is capable of functioning efficiently, accomplishing the necessary "regulation" on its own. Consider the for-profit sector, which has by far the worst record of loan repayments and lack of student persistence. Are the gainful employment regulations necessary? Or could the DOE rely simply upon loan repayment rates as a surrogate for student success in postgraduation employment? I think the latter is the right answer. Apparently, Secretary DeVos agrees:

Continuing to deliver on her promise of a regulatory reset at the Department of Education, U.S. Secretary of Education Betsy DeVos announced today the Department will allow additional time for institutions to comply with overly burdensome Gainful Employment regulations.

"Since their creation under the previous administration, Gainful Employment regulations have been repeatedly challenged by educational institutions and overturned by the courts, underscoring the need for a regulatory reset," said Secretary DeVos. "We need to get this right for our students, and we need to get this right for our institutions of higher education. Once fully implemented, the current rules would unfairly and arbitrarily limit students' ability to pursue certain types of higher education and career training programs. We need to expand, not limit, paths to higher education for students, while also continuing to hold accountable those institutions that do not serve students well."

The Department will now give higher education institutions until July 1, 2018, to comply with disclosure requirements originally due on July 1, 2017, regarding the distribution of gainful employment data to students and in promotional materials. The Department is also extending the deadline for programs to file alternate earnings appeals in light of the Court Order in American Association of Cosmetology Schools v. DeVos. A Federal Register notice will be issued within the next 30 days to specifically implement the Court Order and will include information on establishing a new deadline for earnings appeals.

On June 14, 2017, the Department announced it would engage in negotiated rulemaking on Gainful Employment to develop new regulations that would better serve students and enable institutions to provide high-quality programs. (Department of Education)

Going by what may turn out to be a giant step farther, DeVos has suggested that the venerable, and often venerated, Higher Education Act of 1965 not be renewed when it sunsets soon (Harris I). The secretary is not out there all alone. Other critics of the HEA, such as Senator Lamar Alexander, point out, "A new law could present lawmakers with the opportunity to fix several lingering issues such as student debt, accreditation, shortfalls in institutional funding, and the data that students and families use to make decisions about attending college" (Harris II).

In writing these words, I recognize that our industry (a word many readers reject at the threshold) is dominated by liberals. On most issues, I test "liberal" myself...honest, I'm a lifelong Democrat. However, I'm a Democrat who voted twice for Ronald Reagan. And I'm a Democrat who is willing to give the devil his due. If deregulation will help us survive the Fifth-Wave tsunami, and perhaps even prosper—namely by remaining one of America's few "world-beaters" in the flat-earth global marketplace—then I favor deregulation...even if it's accomplished by Lucifer.

Of course, economic/financial considerations don't account for all federal regulatory activity. Much regulation of our industry is driven not by dollars, but by ethical and moral considerations. The best—and to my mind, most controversial—example of this tendency to make our campuses the *loci* of a moral crusade is the recent campaign to stamp out sexual assaults. I broached this topic in Chapter Five. There I laid out the problem, which is two-fold: the "conviction"[1] of the accused without benefit of a full measure of due process, and the disruption of our institutions by the resulting lawsuits! Now I want to explore solutions.

Reversing the "Sexual Assault" Debacle

Let me acknowledge here that I accept unreservedly that the crusaders against campus sexual assault are sincere in their positions and honest in their efforts. However, Johnson and Taylor's book and the articles and blogs and op eds which have flowed from it raise questions that attorneys and other advocates of civil liberties cannot in good conscience ignore.

In Chapter Five, I suggested that Title IX stands out, even from among the other massive regulatory burdens imposed upon higher education. So, certain am I on this point from hard personal experience complimented by research, that I am prepared to put forward the following policy recommendations for consideration:

- The federal government, and specifically the DOE and DOJ, should revisit their interpretation, regulation, and enforcement of Title IX as it relates to sexual assault. (As this book goes to press this appears to be happening.)
- At a bare minimum, the government should require that the standard of proof in on-campus sexual assault cases be raised to "clear weight of the evidence," as against "more likely than not." If the government won't do it, we should do it ourselves, even if it incurs the wrath of the DOE Office of Civil Rights.
- The same may be said of the other rights of the accused that I identify in Table 5.1 of Chapter Five.
- Ideally, our federal government should do one of two things: either put sexual assaults exclusively back in the hands of our public law enforcement agencies, or if that is not politically possible, then amend Title IX to give higher education a blanket immunity from civil suits by disappointed

accusers and accused alike. This immunity should extend to university employees as well. Either of these outcomes is a result worthy of our lobbying efforts.
- So long as the responsibility to play police, judge, and jury in these cases persists, higher education administrators should consider diverting some of the funds and human resources devoted to enforcement into self-defense training for female staff, faculty, and students, who should be strongly encouraged to participate. This last suggestion derives from success reported by universities that have tried it (University of Oregon).

Colleagues who hope to "Make Title IX Our Own" (Brown) might step outside their envelopes and consider supporting some of these suggestions.

The DeVos DOE appears prepared to pursue something like this path. A mid-June 2017 memo from Candice Jackson, acting assistant secretary for civil rights, to her OCR crew commands,

> Effective immediately, there is no mandate that any one type of complaint is automatically treated differently than any other type of complaint with respect to the scope of the investigation, the type or amount of data needed to conduct the investigation, or the amount or type of review or oversight needed over the investigation by headquarters. (Harris III)

This initial volley was followed by retraction of the 2011 "Dear Colleague" letter that started it all and issuance of interim guidance pending new regulations, as this book went to press. (FIRE)

Note

1. One may take issue with my use of the word "conviction." No, the accused found responsible in a campus-adjudication is not convicted of a crime and will not be sent to prison... not as a result of the university's investigation and adjudication at any rate. This is not to say that the accused, who is found responsible by a preponderance of the evidence (more likely than not), does not endure severe consequences. The severity of the consequences of such an outcome no doubt explains the proliferation of subsequent lawsuits grounded upon defamation and related tort claims against the investigators and adjudicators.

References

AACSB, "About Us," accessed at http://www.aacsb.edu/about.
ABC News, "Lost in America: Visa Program Struggles to Track Missing Foreign Students," September 2, 2014, accessed at http://abcnews.go.com/Blotter/visa-program-struggles-track-missing-foreign-students/story?id=25208740
Annenberg Public Policy Center, "9/11 Hijackers and Student Visas," FactCheck.org, November 24, 2015, accessed at http://www.factcheck.org/2013/05/911-hijackers-and-student-visas/
Bradner, Eric and Rene Marsh, "Acting TSA Director Reassigned, After Screeners Failed Tests to Detect Explosives, Weapons," CNN, June 2, 2015, accessed at http://www.cnn.com/2015/06/01/politics/tsa-failed-undercover-airport-screening-tests/
Brown, Sarah, "In the Time of Trump, Colleges Start to 'Make Title IX Our Own'," *Chronicle of Higher Education*, June 25, 2017.
Clark, Adam, "N.J. to Require More Classroom Time for Student Teachers," NJ.com, November 5, 2015, accessed at http://www.nj.com/education/2015/11/nj_to_require_more_classroom_time_for_student_teac.html
Department of Education, "DeVos Pressed Pause on Burdensome Gainful Employment Regulations," June 30, 2017, accessed at https://www.ed.gov/news/press-releases/devos-presses-pause-burdensome-gainful-employment-regulations
Ellucian, accessed at http://www.ellucian.com/landing-pages/download-white-paper-campus-tech-forge-a-personal-connection/?utm_source=bing&utm_medium=cpc&utm_campaign=Brand&utm_term=degreeworks&utm_content=Degree%20Works
Ellucian International Student and Scholar Management, accessed at http://www.ellucian.com/Solution-Sheets/Ellucian-International-Student-and-Scholar-Management/
Fain, Paul, "J-Schools Dump Accreditor," *Inside Higher Ed*, May 3, 2017, accessed at https://www.insidehighered.com/news/2017/05/03/northwestern-and-berkeleys-journalism-schools-drop-accreditor-echoing-broader?utm_source=Inside+Higher+Ed&utm_campaign=f4dd856ab9-DNU20170503&utm_medium=email&utm_term=0_1fcbc04421-f4dd856ab9-198501157&mc_cid=f4dd856ab9&mc_eid=73be4d9bca
Fain, Paul (Fain II), "Trump Administration Backs Termination of ACICS," *Inside Higher Ed*, May 2, 2017, accessed at https://www.insidehighered.com/quicktakes/2017/05/02/trump-administration-backs-termination-acics
Federation for American Immigration Reform (FAIR), "Identity and Immigration Status of 9/11 Terrorists," Immigration Issues (2011) accessed at http://www.fairus.org/issue/identity-and-immigration-status-of-9-11-terrorists
FIRE (Foundation for Individual Rights in Education), "Dear Colleague: It's Over! Education Department Rescinds Controversial 2011 Letter," Sept. 22, 2017.
Fischer, Karin, "Canada Capitalizes on a 'Trump Bump'—and Years of Preparation." *Chronicle of Higher Education*, July 18, 2017.
Friedman, Hershey H. and Frimette Kass-Schraibman, "The Ethics of AACSB Accreditation: Unintended Consequences," SSRN, December 20, 2016, accessed at https://papers.ssrn.com/sol3/papers.cfm?abstract_id=2887096

Harris, Adam (I), "Landmark Law on Higher Education Should Be Scrapped, DeVos Suggests," *Chronicle of Higher Education*, June 21, 2017.

Harris, Adam (II), "What Would the Repeal of Higher Ed's Foundational Law Mean for Colleges?" *Chronicle of Higher Education*, June 23, 2017.

Harris, Adam (III), "Memo Outlines Education Dept. Plans to Scale Back Civil-Rights Efforts," *Chronicle of Higher Education*, June 15, 2017.

Iasevoll, Brenda, "Trump Signs Bill Scrapping Teacher-Prep Rules," *Education Week*, March 28, 2017, accessed at http://blogs.edweek.org/edweek/teacherbeat/2017/03/trump_signs_bill_scrapping_tea.html (The proposed regulations may be accessed at https://www2.ed.gov/documents/teaching/teacher-prep-final-regs.pdf)

IIE, Project Atlas, accessed at https://www.iie.org/en/Research-and-Insights/Project-Atlas

Moran, Melanie, "Study Estimates Cost of Regulatory Compliance at 13 Colleges and Universities," *Vanderbilt News*, October 19, 2015, accessed at https://news.vanderbilt.edu/2015/10/19/regulatory-compliance/

Presidential Executive Order on Reducing Regulation and Controlling Regulatory Costs, January 30, 2017, accessed at https://www.whitehouse.gov/the-press-office/2017/01/30/presidential-executive-order-reducing-regulation-and-controlling

Rider University, "ESL Programs/ On Campus Plus," accessed at http://www.rider.edu/admissions/international/how-to-apply/esl-on-campus-plus

Sawchuck, Stephen, "Teacher Education Group Airs Criticism of New Accreditor," *Education Week*, March 17, 2015, accessed at http://www.edweek.org/ew/articles/2015/03/18/teacher-education-group-airs-criticism-of-new.html

University of Oregon, "Are Women Safer When They Learn Self-Defense?" *Cascade*, Spring 2013, accessed at https://cascade.uoregon.edu/spring2013/social-sciences/are-women-safer-when-they-learn-self-defense/

U.S. *News & World Report*, "Best Business Schools," accessed at https://www.usnews.com/best-graduate-schools/top-business-schools/mba-rankings

WBUR, "More International Students Uneasy About Studying in the U.S.," February 28, 2017, accessed at http://www.wbur.org/hereandnow/2017/02/28/international-students-uneasy-us

Westervelt, Eric, "Where Have All the Teachers Gone?", National Public Radio, March 3, 2015, accessed at http://www.npr.org/sections/ed/2015/03/03/389282733/where-have-all-the-teachers-gone

Wikipedia, "List of Business Schools in the United States," accessed at https://en.wikipedia.org/wiki/List_of_business_schools_in_the_United_States

· 9 ·

SOME REAL-WORLD SOLUTIONS

For more than two decades, I have been the Associate Provost and Legal Counsel for Academic Affairs at Rider University in Lawrenceville, New Jersey. During my most recent year there, I was a member of the leadership team grappling with an existential financial crisis, along the lines of those outlined in Chapter Five. Rider's 150-plus years span all but the first wave in the history of American higher education. Its history also subsumes two of the three sectors of higher education into which I delved in detail in Part One: the for-profit and the not-for-profit private sectors. And, most importantly, in my most-proximate years at Rider, I was a witness to a Fifth-Wave financial crisis representative of the mega-crisis shaking the foundations of American higher education…and a participant in Rider's efforts to meet the challenge.

Rider is in its deepest roots an example of entrepreneurship at the end of the American Civil War. Henry Bryant, Henry Stratton, and William Whitney founded the Trenton Business College on October 2, 1865, in anticipation of the interest of returning veterans in a business education. In that motivation for its founding, Rider prefigures the Fourth-Wave surge in higher education aimed at meeting the needs of returning veterans of World War II exactly 80 years later. Indeed, Bryant and Stratton had been engaged since 1853 in building the chain of for-profit business schools that survives to this very day in half-a-dozen states and online (Bryant & Stratton).

Although, as we've seen, the Second Wave of American higher education was dominated by the great public land-grant schools, a "private business school movement percolated in the background. The first such for-profit school was founded by one Benjamin Franklin Foster in Boston in 1827. By 1850 about 20 such schools were scattered around the U.S. Briggs and Stratton started their little empire in Cleveland, Ohio some eight years prior to the War Between the States" (Brower, p. 1).

In 1868, Andrew J. Rider and one Joseph Beecher acquired the school from the Bryant and Stratton organization. The leading historian of Rider's roots is vague about Andrew J.'s background. While a teacher and administrator with the B&S organization, he also owned substantial interests in the cranberry bogs of South Jersey. Suffice to say that the man had money and by 1873 had acquired sole ownership of what predictably became the Rider Business College (Brower, p. 9).

Twenty years later, Andrew J.'s cranberry empire demanded most of his time and attention. And, so, he took on a partner, Franklin Benjamin Moore, late of the Cedar Rapids Business College. In 1898, Moore took over the presidency and bought out A.J. Rider. His son, Franklin Frazee Moore, would succeed him in 1934. Taken together, they would lead the college for some eight decades, until the late 1960s (Rider).

During the first third of the 20th century, the college won the right to grant bachelor degrees and added a school of education. During this growth period, Rider remained a for-profit entity. The college also remained remarkably resilient during the Great Depression. The accession of Moore the Younger to the presidency marked a momentous departure, from for-profit to nonprofit status, followed by accreditation under the umbrella of the Middle States Accrediting Association (Brower, pp. 61–67).

The school's resilience has been attributed to its focus on practical skills and its streamlined curriculum (Brower, pp. 61–67). Its switch to nonprofit status was likely motivated by changes in the federal tax code during the New Deal and a desire for the mantle of legitimacy afforded by Middle States accreditation.

The next big change began in 1956, when the college bought a 300+ acre farm in Lawrenceville, a small town some eight miles from Trenton. Once again, though the Fourth Wave would be dominated by the mushrooming megaversities of post-World War II, Rider College rose with the rest of higher ed's many boats. By 1964, the Rider College relocation was complete. The institution was comprised of business, education, graduate, and liberal arts schools, plus an evening division (Rider).

The Moore Dynasty would wind down in the late 1960s. The transition climaxed with the hiring of Dr. Frank Elliott, provost of Hofstra University, as only the fourth president of Rider College. Elliott inherited the helm during an era of upheaval within and outside of American higher education. During the sixties and early seventies, the ever-practical Rider College saw little of the SDS, the war protests, or flower power. What it did see, however, was the faculty unionization movement, which was in full swing in higher education, as Elliott wrestled with issues of tenure (or more accurately, tenure denied or indefinitely delayed).

The successful organizing drive of the American Association of University Professors, culminating in an NLRB-supervised election, has been fully documented elsewhere (Begin) and need not be recounted here. Suffice to say that the outcome was a faculty–professional librarian–athletic coach union of ever-increasing strength and influence at Rider College. So strong was the Rider Chapter of the AAUP by 1980 that the U.S. Supreme Court's ruling (*Yeshiva University*), that tenured faculty are managers who fall outside the shield of the National Labor Relations Act, failed to trigger a withdrawal of recognition by the Rider administration, in sharp contrast to such de-unionization steps at numerous other private colleges and universities.

Consequently, by the time I was hired in the fall of 1996, Rider (renamed a university a few years earlier at the same time that it acquired the Westminster Choir College in Princeton) epitomized the concept of "joint governance." Even today, the collective bargaining agreement between Rider University and the AAUP runs to 200+ pages and doubles as a faculty handbook. While most universities had a faculty senate that recommended policies to the administration, Rider was (and is) governed by academic policy committees dominated by faculty members. The provost could (and can) refuse to enact a policy passed by a school or college APC only for a very limited number of reasons enumerated specifically in the labor contract.

That contract typically ran for three years, after which the parties returned to the negotiating table. The union so contrived the summer renegotiation process that the issues of wages and benefits were only reached in September, when the students were back on campus and a strike was a "nuclear option" that the administration dreaded. Consequently, faculty wages and benefits grew like Topsy, until by the second decade of the 21st century, Rider's cost of delivering instruction surpassed that of virtually all of its competitors.

This cost-of-instruction gap yawned particularly wide at the choir college in Princeton, some eight miles from the main campus in Lawrenceville. While Rider's cost of delivering a course credit was out of whack with its competition, both private and public, the average cost per credit at the music school, due chiefly to one-on-one vocal lessons, was a dramatic outlier even internally.

Finally, in the fall of 2015, a new president, who discovered a deepening deficit when he took the helm, demanded wage concessions from the union. When the AAUP declined, Dr. Gregory Dell'Omo declared the first faculty lay off in the school's 150-year history. Shocked into awareness, the union leadership folded and acquiesced to removing two pending wage increases from the 2014–2017 collective agreement.

This concession staunched the bleeding partly, but not enough. Although the parties were scheduled to return to the bargaining table in the summer of '17, the university initiated a new round of concessionary bargaining in 2016. These talks were inconclusive, petering out in January 2017. But they set the stage and tone for the regular negotiations in the summer.

Meanwhile, a board-mandated study group determined that Rider University could no longer afford the luxury of its "uptown address." The decision was made and it was announced to sell the Westminster Choir College, either as an ongoing concern or piecemeal, the property to one buyer and the music programs to somebody else (Seltzer I). The decision caused a furor among faculty, students, alumni, and supporters of WCC. Those intent on preventing the divestiture formed a "Save Westminster" movement driven by the social media. By June 2017, its leadership had launched a legal challenge in the U.S. District Court for eastern New York (Seltzer II).

Meanwhile, the plan to save Rider from the threat of possible insolvency was constructed as a three-legged stool: significant concessions from the AAUP, sale of WCC, and bringing in a robust freshman class. This latter leg was honed along the lines I suggest in Chapter Six: shooting with a rifle rather than a shotgun with regard to tuition discounting. The tactic worked in attracting a healthy number of new students…in fact a class in excess of 1,000, one of the largest in Rider's history. While it required an aggregate dip below the tuition sticker price in excess of 50 percent, net profits proved adequate to bear their share of operating expenses.

In summer 2017, I was a member of the four-man negotiating team bargaining with the AAUP for multi-million-dollar concessions in wages and benefits. And the call for proposals for purchasing the choir college attracted some two dozen responses, which went under review by a joint trustee/administrator committee. And, third, the University's collective fingers were crossed that no significant "melt" will diminish the incoming student population in September, a wish that was realized.

The outcome of this three-pronged Rider initiative is not as important as the point I have already implied in my telling of the tale: saving nonprofit private schools like Rider can be an exercise in attrition: reductions in staff size through normal (or abnormal) staff attrition, combined with concomitant cuts in payrolls and employee benefits; divestiture of unprofitable academic programs and physical assets; deep tuition discounts.

My institution's three-pronged attack on its deficit appears to be succeeding. As noted above, in fall 2017 Rider admitted one of its largest freshman classes ever. I can report, without violating confidences, that at the bargaining table our team achieved substantial concessions from the AAUP (Rider AAUP). And, according to public sources, the university entered talks with a potential buyer interested in acquiring and operating the choir college (Koller).

Is Rider safely ashore? No, not yet…but its head is above water. It is not bleeding cash reserves. It is embarking on new, popular academic programs, such as business analytics, computer science, and criminal justice. An influx of fresh cash from a Westminster sale could help enable still more substantial initiatives.

A Unique Response to the Facilities Arms Race

Here's another story I can personalize a little. When I was a student in the late 1960s at Lancaster (PA)'s Franklin & Marshall College, which was then all-male, women were bussed in for homecoming weekend from nearby all-female colleges. Goucher in nearby Maryland was one of these.

Goucher, like F&M, ceased its uni-sex approach to higher education not very long after I graduated in 1969. However, down the decades, Goucher's students, male and female, continued to reside in dorms dating from those all-female days. Intended to protect the "girls" from prying eyes, Goucher's campus featured walls and courtyards that some say gave it a prison-like feel. The residence halls themselves are circa 1950s (Biemiller).

Students expect better, especially at the price tags private schools place on tuition, room & board. To build new residence halls that meet market demands, Goucher's administration faced a $16-million investment challenge. Instead of floating bonds in order to borrow the capital, the college leaders and the Baltimore architects they hired came up with an $8-million "green" solution. They moved the three fifties-vintage buildings down a slope to a new, more attractive location and fully refurbished them. And they did it all in the single summer of 2017, so that the digs were ready for occupancy in September (Biemiller).

Originally the Woman's College of Baltimore, Goucher was founded by a minister for whom the school was renamed in 1910. For moving its dorms around the way one might move castles on a chess board suggests, the college has been named a top-ten innovator by *U.S. News & World Report*. It claims on its website, "A highlight of Goucher's unique liberal arts curriculum is the requirement that all undergraduates must study abroad at least once before graduation, making the college the first in the nation to make such a bold move in globalized education" (Goucher). Well, that's not quite accurate. Denison College, near Harrisburg (PA) tried this sort of curricular mandate several decades ago with mixed results. Sending its juniors abroad meant that, when they returned with a diminished sense of connection to the college, there was a vacuum of senior-class leadership on campus. That, as much as anything, led to abandonment of the model. Goucher seems to have opted for a more flexible approach, which may work well. No matter…give the school's leadership points for innovation, all the same.

Moving the residence halls, instead of demolishing them, is the green and financially frugal solution of Facilities Director Terence McCann Jr., who explained, "I wasn't there when the decision was made to demolish them. I walked into the Whiting-Turner trailer one day and asked, What do you think about a few other options" (Biemiller).

Requiring students to study abroad is a complimentary move. It allows for enrollment growth, while yet again avoiding capital investment in more residence halls. This, then, is yet another small example of how those institutions most at risk in the Fifth Wave can creatively avoid drowning.

Tuition in the School of Hard Knocks

I will go further. The Rider and Goucher stories are emblematic of the kinds of "real world" solutions that cash-strapped, struggling middle-of-the-pack colleges and universities must embrace, absent a dramatic influx of big money from a mega-bucks donor wishing to grasp the ultimate naming opportunity (e.g., Rowan University, formerly a mediocre state school that received $100 million from aging industrialist Hank Rowan).

The lead in a 2017 *Inside Higher Ed* article reads, "Tuition discounting at private colleges and universities is up again. Tuition revenue is straining to keep up. And enrollment is weak" (Seltzer III). About a year earlier, the *Washington Post* said that tuition discounting might represent a "race to extinction." The article noted, "In the retail and restaurant worlds, the strategy among the likes of Walmart and McDonald's has long been to gain market share with seemingly endless discounts. But that approach is showing signs of aging as consumer preferences shift and lower prices weigh on the bottom line."

The piece continues,

> The same is now true for higher education. Most colleges and universities have managed to fill their classes each year by employing sophisticated discounting strategies that extended cut-rate tuition rates to just enough students to encourage them to enroll. In the past decade those discounts not only have gotten much bigger, but schools offered them to more students—including those who used to pay full price—to entice them to campus. (Selingo)

Hand-in-hand with deep discounts is the continuous launching of new programs. At Rider health science and musical theater also have been popular new entrants into the curriculum. The trouble is that, to repeat yet again Gilbert and Sullivan lyric in "The Gondoliers," "When everybody's somebody, then nobody's anybody."

The same may be said of campus facilities. If every school creates the equivalent of a "college town" concept, then no college has an advantage… only larger debt service.

And, finally, with regard to the high hopes I expressed in Chapter Eight regarding regulatory relief, even that seems more elusive than I anticipated. Most notably, while I was right to predict that Secretary of Education DeVos would back away from Obama-era enforcement of Title IX in sexual-assault cases (DOE I), the DOE's Office of Civil Rights continues its enforcement activities unabated (DOE II).

This example is illustrative of what many are labeling "the deep state," i.e., the entrenched federal bureaucracy that apparently is digging in and resisting the Trump Administration's efforts at top-down deregulation. One writer observes,

> By my count, the current usage of "deep state," as it supposedly relates to Trump's troubles, entails three overlapping understandings: The first has to do with war, militarism, and intelligence, the secret institutions that have deep roots but were fused together in a powerful way under the administrations of George W. Bush and Barack Obama (Marc Ambinder's book, Deep State, along with this recent essay in Foreign Policy, are good guides); the second with private corporate power, especially associated with finance, the arms trade, and fossil fuels; and the third with the many embedded bureaucrats of the US government's many administrative agencies, who, we hope, are leading a passive resistance to Trump's program of privatization and deregulation. (Grandin)

Of course, it's the third category with which I am concerned here. As a life-long Democrat and (on most issues) a liberal, I join the author in hoping that this embedded bureaucracy will successfully resist the Trump Administration's deregulation crusade in such areas as the environment, healthcare, and workplace safety. However, as my Chapter Eight indicates, I find myself conflicted. As illustrated in that chapter, accreditation, regulation of international students[1], financial-aid monitoring, even animal welfare regulations, and a plethora of other rules and regs combine to create an increasingly unmanageable administrative burden. More significantly, they interfere with our access to a potentially game-changing global market of new students and expose us to potentially existential legal, financial, and PR liabilities. Imagine a surfer trying to ride the Fifth Wave with a very large albatross hanging around the neck.

Meanwhile, as I predicted in Chapter Four, it's the for-profit sector of higher ed that thus far is the big winner under the Trump/DeVos regime, as the Obama Administration's hard-won "gainful employment" regulations are shelved (DOE III).

So…how much hope is there for the weak sisters in the higher education family…the small- and midsized private colleges caught in the tuition-discount death spiral and the middling public universities out of favor with their legislators?

Undoubtedly, some will be swamped by the Fifth Wave.

However, if that were my bottom line, you might fairly accuse me of false advertising. After all, the subtitle of this little volume is "a survival guide for the new normal."

So what then? First, I recommend that you take applicable ideas outlined in Chapters Six through this chapter to heart. Implement any and all that will work for your institution.

Second, and I think more importantly, if you are in the position to do so—if you are what's currently called a "thought leader" in your college or university—then think outside the box (your ideas may be much better than mine). Yes, I am well aware that many academics hate thinking of their schools as businesses. They hate thinking of their students as customers. This, nevertheless, is my bottom line.

A university is an enterprise comprised of a collection of assets, including a physical plant, another fixed asset known as the tenured faculty (as permanent and expensive as the machinery in a factory), an endowment (unique in the industrial world in one sense, but not unlike cash reserves if viewed from a different angle), an entertainment division (athletics, music, theater, faculty super-stars, etc.), and a management team.

Viewed like this, a college or university as enterprise, the goal should be to turn a profit. A former Rider president was fond of saying, "We're not for-profit...but we're not for loss." Viewed like this, a university shouldn't worry too much about how it earns a buck—provided it protects its brand, abides by traditional ideals such as academic freedom, and respects the rule of the law.

Some Additional Ideas

Inefficient practices should be abolished. For example, the ritual of the executive search, which supports a whole head-hunter industry on the custom that all members of the campus community must have a voice in the choice of president, provost, vice presidents, and deans should be compressed. In the Fifth Wave world of lay-offs and pay freezes, nobody below the president and the cabinet believes that all inclusive searches are time well-spent. Believe me. Stop wasting human and financial resources on such arcane rituals.

If you haven't moved to a profit-center model, seriously consider doing so now. Programs that turn a profit, or have potential to do so, should be sustained and nurtured. Programs that don't should go. This means, you have to engage in periodic prioritization exercises. Prioritization is a much better expenditure of resources, human and monetary, than either programmatic accreditation or campus-wide strategic planning.

Foster an attitude among your faculty that they actually hold full-time jobs. Full-time means being on campus five days a week. It means teaching at least four courses a semester. It means identifying and pursuing grant and contract opportunities. It means sharing ownership of recruitment and retention.

Inventory your assets. Are they being used productively 12 months a year? Stop talking in terms of the "academic year," and start talking about the calendar or fiscal year.

Beyond an inventory of physical plant, inventory intellectual property. And ask, who owns the intellectual property? If a faculty member writes a book or composes music or writes software, should this be the instructor's intellectual property? All too often we answer yes, and then shrug when told that faculty in the humanities and social sciences have only limited opportunities to bring in auxiliary (defined here as nontuition) cash flow. Perhaps royalties ought to be shared.

Absent the rare *deus ex machina* (e.g., Hank Rowan of Rowan University), the solutions are incremental. They are cumulative. They are small victories that add up and, hopefully, bring a result that is greater than the sum of its component parts. That is the "magical" element of a truly successful college or university. It can't be quantified or measured. It's qualitative and can only be felt. It is the essence of the truly successful institution and, like the tree of liberty, it must be watered by every successive generation. This is a persistent watering, as contrasted to the Fifth-Wave tsunami.

I see no persuasive reason why a college, regardless of size of student body or size of endowment or size of physical plant, cannot ride the Fifth Wave to the shores of survival and success. The key in my opinion lies in the palms of all our hands. First, as I am at pains to do in the Introduction and first chapter, we must recognize that the Fifth Wave carries a profound paradigm shift, not unlike the altered weather pattern arising from global warming that has made the 2017 hurricane season the worst in recorded history. Second we must recognize that such profound paradigm shifts demand concomitant perceptual shifts in the minds and visions of the leaders who must navigate their enterprises through the storm such a wave churns up.

There it is: the challenge and some solutions. Can you ride the wave and rise to the challenge? Or will you cling to the wreckage of arcane norms, customs, and practices…and drown?

Note

1. As if intent on making matters worse, President Trump's relentless series of Executive Orders aimed at restricting travel to the United States from predominantly Muslim nations, scares off students who hitherto have been a boon to schools such as my own, which offer ESL programs as a path to matriculation.

References

Begin, James P., Theodore Settle and Paula Becker Alexander, *Academics on Strike* (New Brunswick, NJ: Rutgers University Press 1975).

Biemiller, Lawrence, "Need Dorms? Here's One College's 'Crazy' Idea to Recycle 3 Buildings," *Chronicle of Higher Education*, July 20, 2017.

Brower, Walter Ashley, Jr., *Rider College: The First One Hundred Years* (Trenton, NJ: privately published 1965).

Bryant & Stratton College, "Locations," May 14, 2017, accessed at https://www.bryantstratton.edu/locations

Department of Education (DOE I), "Department of Education Issues New Interim Guidance on Campus Sexual Misconduct," U.S. Department of Education, September 22, 2017, accessed at https://www.ed.gov/news/press-releases/department-education-issues-new-interim-guidance-campus-sexual-misconduct

Department of Education (DOE II), "U.S. Education Department Reaches Agreement with Wittenberg University Concerning Title IX Violations," U.S. Department of Education, March 24, 2017, accessed at https://www.ed.gov/news/press-releases/us-education-department-reaches-agreement-wittenberg-university-concerning-title-ix-violations

Department of Education (DOE III), "DeVos Presses Pause on Burdensome Gainful Employment Regulations, U.S. Department of Education, June 30, 2017, accessed at https://www.ed.gov/news/press-releases/devos-presses-pause-burdensome-gainful-employment-regulations

Goucher College, "Who We Are," accessed at http://www.goucher.edu/about/who-we-are

Grandin, Greg, "What Is the Deep State?" *The Nation*, February 17, 2017, accessed at https://www.thenation.com/article/what-is-the-deep-state/

Koller, Matt, "Who Were Today's WCC Visitors?" *Coalition to Save Westminster Choir College in Princeton, Inc.*, October 3, 2017, accessed at https://www.savewestminster.org/matt-koller-who-were-todays-visitors/

Rider University, "Historic Timeline," May 14, 2017, accessed at http://www.rider.edu/about-rider/historic-rider/historic-timeline

Rider University Chapter of the AAUP, "Tentative Agreement," September 5, 2017, accessed at http://www.rideraaup.net/

Selingo, Jeffrey J., "Colleges Heavily Discount Tuition, and It Might be a Race to Extinction," *The Washington Post*, May 16, 2016.

Seltzer, Rick (Seltzer I), "Selling Off a College," *Inside Higher Ed*, April 7, 2017, accessed at https://www.insidehighered.com/news/2017/04/07/rider-university-plows-new-ground-westminster-choir-college-sale

Seltzer, Rick (Seltzer II), "Westminster College Backers Sue Rider," *Inside Higher Ed*, June 22, 2017, accessed at https://www.insidehighered.com/quicktakes/2017/06/22/westminster-choir-college-backers-sue-rider

Seltzer, Rick (Seltzer III), "Private Colleges and Universities Increase Tuition Discounting Again in 2016–17," *Inside Higher Ed*, May 15, 2017, accessed at https://www.insidehighered.com/news/2017/05/15/private-colleges-and-universities-increase-tuition-discounting-again-2016-17

Yeshiva University, NLRB v., 444 U.S. 672 (1980).

www.ingramcontent.com/pod-product-compliance
Ingram Content Group UK Ltd.
Pitfield, Milton Keynes, MK11 3LW, UK
UKHW021326180426
11947UKWH00017B/1464